2021 Happy Birthday. 10 yrs Everett old !!

Lots of information to answer all your questions - you can inform your Dad!

Love you - Your Nana and Papa

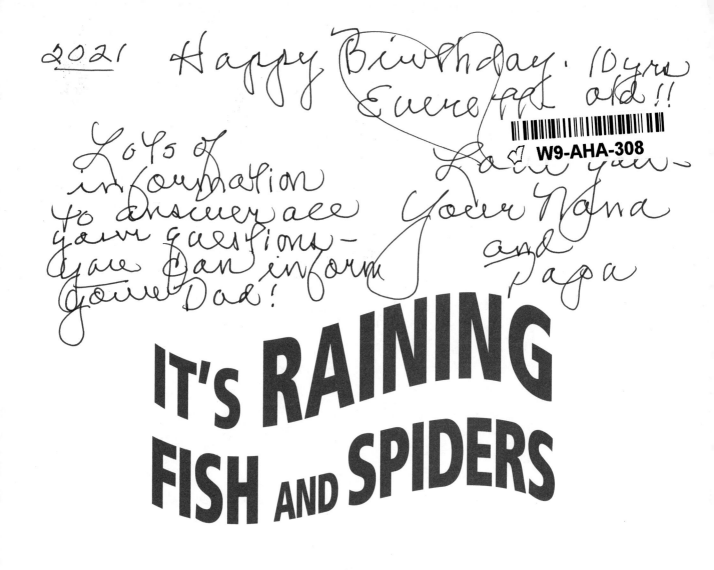

IT'S RAINING FISH AND SPIDERS

BILL EVANS

IT'S RAINING FISH AND SPIDERS

A TOM DOHERTY ASSOCIATES BOOK
NEW YORK

IT'S RAINING FISH AND SPIDERS

A Forge Book
Published by Tom Doherty Associates, LLC
175 Fifth Avenue
New York, NY 10010

www.tor-forge.com

Forge® is a registered trademark of Tom Doherty Associates, LLC.

ISBN 978-0-7653-2132-9

First Edition: May 2012

Printed in the United States of America

0 9 8 7 6 5 4 3 2

· Contents ·

CONTENTS

SECTION 3:

Blizzards

CONTENTS

SECTION 4:
Extreme Weather!

CONTENTS

CONTENTS

. Author's Note .

I haven't had a bad day since the doctor slapped me on the behind!

I have been very fortunate and blessed. I was fortunate to be raised by my loving, caring grandparents, and blessed by the grace of God to be where I am in life today. I have also been very fortunate to have met some truly great human beings along the way—people who helped me with my career. Others, devoted to meteorology, were of great help to me in the creation of this book.

I want to begin by thanking two people who believed in me enough to give me the once-in-a-lifetime opportunities that led me to where I am today: the late Don Partridge of what was then WDAL AM/FM radio and Bob Holland, weatherman and station manager of WTOK-TV, both in Meridian, Mississippi.

The radio job Don gave me when I was thirteen years old laid the foreground for my broadcasting career. I hung around the station and learned how to be a true broadcaster: reading news, weather, and sports; playing music; ad-libbing live commercial copy; and doing live radio remotes. Thanks to Don and

his son, Mike Partridge, for all that training and for beating me into shape.

Bob Holland gave me my first television job when I returned to Meridian after college. He was the first TV weatherman in our town— and he spent his whole career there. He could have easily moved on to one of the bigger networks but he chose to homestead in Meridian. Bob had a deep, deep, bass voice that was tremendously soothing and comforting to hear coming from the TV when tornadoes were threatening to destroy our town. I wanted to be just like Bob, and I was lucky that he became my mentor. I would drop by and visit/pester Bob about being a weatherman when I was in high school. He gave me incredibly valuable advice about career and job choices, and went on to give me my first chance in TV news. Thanks, Bob, you'll always be my hero.

The other person I want to thank is Stewart Kellogg, currently general manager of WAPT-TV in Jackson, Mississippi. When Stu filled the main weather position while he was news director at WALA-TV in Mobile, Alabama, he whittled the list of candidates down to two—me and some other guy. It was a tight contest and Stu kept playing both audition tapes to anyone who would watch, even the teller at his local bank!

To my eternal gratitude, he eventually chose me! Stu was a great boss and a great person. He taught me a lot about broadcast TV and truly launched me toward my career in New York City. See, I told you I was blessed and fortunate. Surround yourself with great people and you'll go far in your career and in life.

Next, I want to thank Melissa Ann Singer of Tor/Forge Books for her amazing editing, encouragement, and foresight. She loves weather, is a weather junkie like me, and is a sweetheart. There is not a dog on Earth that would bite her. She is the best—as are all the staff at Tor who have been so wonderful to me and such visionaries on this project. In a meeting about my first two novels, *Category 7* and *Frozen Fire*, I mentioned my desire to do this book. They didn't even bat an eye, just jumped right in on the project. They shared my commitment to publishing a great, fun book on extreme weather for kids.

This is a big dream of mine, to write an exciting book about weather to excite a new generation of future meteorologists. The people at Tor/Forge have no idea what they've unleashed!

Special thanks to all these people at Tor/Forge, who helped my dreams become reality: Kathleen Doherty, Susan Chang, and Juliet Pederson of the young adult publishing division, without whom this book would not exist; Seth Lerner and Vanessa Paolantonio, who designed the cover for this book; Pauline Neuwirth and Nathan Weaver of production; Phyllis Azar and her talented team in ad/promo; Alexis Saarela in publicity; and everyone in sales and marketing, especially the sales reps who got this book into your hands.

And of course, my undying thanks to Linda Quinton, vice president and associate publisher, and Tom Doherty, president and publisher, who have supported me since my very first steps into the world of book publishing.

I want to thank my lovely wife, Dana, who was also an editor on this book. Dana's an Ivy Leaguer who is much smarter than me. She offered me fantastic input. She also helped keep the kids away so I could bury myself in this project.

To my agent, Coleen O'Shea, "The World's Greatest Book Agent," thanks so much for believing in my ideas. You are so supportive and have been fantastic for my publishing career. Thanks for getting me the millions in advance money for the book! You know I'm kidding—it was really billions!

Now I want to mention all the people who have been of amazing assistance in getting this book done. First, I must thank all the people I talked to at the National Oceanic and Atmospheric Administration (NOAA), who helped me at every turn. They responded quickly to every e-mail and every request. They are the ultimate source for weather information or information on the oceans and the atmosphere. NOAA is also the main source for the pictures in this book, most of which come from the NOAA Picture Library.

They are the best in the world at what they do, and if you take a moment to look at their Web site, www.noaa.gov, and materials for learning, you will see why. They really want kids to understand how weather works and they, too, like me, are on a mission to inspire kids to become our next generation of great meteorologists and atmospheric scientists. If you are looking for a great career in weather, you want to get in touch with these folks.

I want to thank the National Weather Service (NWS) for all the years of help they have given me in my career. In my infancy as a weather forecaster, I would go down to the weather service offices in Meridian and Jackson, Mississippi, and the folks at the NWS would teach me about weather. They gave me personal weather briefings that I used in my broadcasts. The NWS is an invaluable asset, and the people there have helped immensely with this project, answering my requests with speed and tons of information. You guys, too, are the best in the world.

I want to thank the Hurricane Hunters for not only taking me on some great rides, but also for returning me home safe and sound! The entire world relies on the Hunters to get the information necessary to make accurate hurricane predictions. You should be commended for your tireless sacrifices as you track monster storms and save lives.

I want to thank Christopher C. Burt, author of *Extreme Weather,* and Jack Williams, author of *The Weather Book.* These fantastic books were *extremely* helpful to me when

I was putting together this *extreme* weather book. You should add their books to your collection along with mine. Thanks also go to Kenneth Libbrecht, whose work with snowflakes is the best in the world.

When I started looking for pictures for this book, I was amazed at the number of people who would let me use their pictures for free. Of course, we gave everyone credit and sent them a copy of the book, but that doesn't seem like much in exchange for their amazing pictures! So I want to thank everyone again—everyone who gave us pictures as part of our endeavor to teach children about the beauty and awe of weather. You should feel very proud about sharing your love of weather with kids, and inspiring them to get excited about the atmosphere. Thanks also to Susan Berkoff for helping me find all the photographers and artists.

I also want to thank the greatest graphic artist since Picasso. Okay, so Picasso wasn't a graphic artist, but Frank Picini is. He made all the great and easy-to-understand graphics in the book. Frank has been doing graphics with me for more than twenty years. He is not only a great designer and artist, but he understands weather! Weather is complicated and Frank makes it a whole lot easier.

Finally, I want to thank the kids. I have been talking to students about the atmosphere for more than thirty years. Kids love weather. They are mesmerized by it. They sponge it up. I love watching their eyes light up when we talk about storms.

I hope this little book inspires you to become some of our next great meteorologists and atmospheric scientists. We need you to keep moving weather forecasting and research forward. We need you to continue to study the skies, help educate the masses, and excite future generations of meteorologists all over the world.

Finally, my advice:

Walk softly, and carry a big umbrella. . . .

IT'S RAINING FISH AND SPIDERS

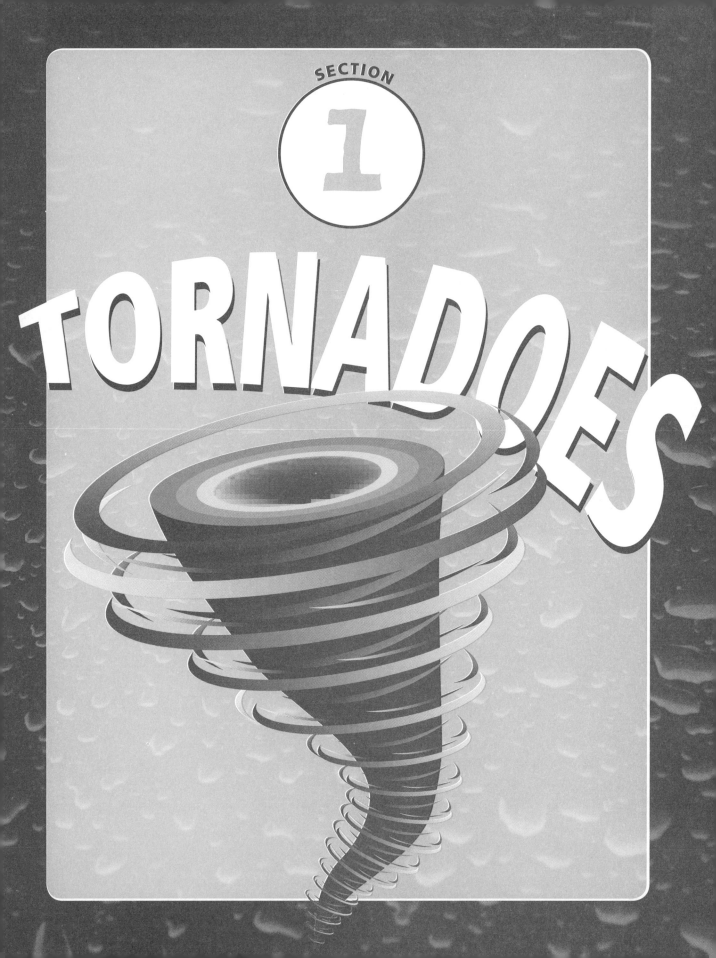

SECTION

1

TORNADOES

What Is a Tornado?

Tornadoes are the most destructive force on the face of the Earth. In terms of "extreme weather," tornadoes are the most awesome, devastating force when you consider how they are created, their various ways of destruction, and the surprising way in which they attack. No other weather phenomenon destroys more property or causes more fatalities than a tornado. Derived from the Spanish word *torna*, meaning "to turn," a tornado is defined as an intense, rotating column of air extending from the base of a thunderstorm cloud to the ground. Tornadoes can strike at any time, appear from any direction, and have hit every state in the United States, including Alaska and Hawaii.

The swirling debris field of a tornado has been clocked to move as fast as nearly 300 miles per hour. Tornado winds have destroyed wind-measuring instruments, caused pine

needles to penetrate bricks, driven straw into trees, and stripped pavement off roads. Tornadoes have caused the roofs of large buildings to be lifted from their frames. The building's walls then fall outward and the roof is dropped back onto the structure, crushing it.

Wood, bricks, pipes, steel, tin siding, cars, tanker trucks, train cars, and even livestock have all been swept up into the storm and carried for miles. There's even one story of the Worcester, Massachusetts, tornado of June 9, 1953, when mattress pieces were carried high into the thunderstorm, when they were coated with ice, before they fell into Boston Harbor.

Unfortunately, people are injured and sometimes killed by tornadoes. In isolated cases, people have been carried as far as a mile from their homes. However, thanks to improved weather forecasting, the use of Doppler radar, and better public awareness, the number of deaths due to tornadoes is fortunately going down.

Another interesting phenomenon of the tornado is its ability to pass over ponds, lakes, or swamps and literally suck up the contents of these bodies of water. At least fifty times a year there are reports of fish, frogs, tadpoles, snakes, eels, or snails dropping from the sky, often landing on unsuspecting people. The debris field is sometimes carried quite high up, into an area where the weather is sunny and nice. As the storm weakens and dissipates, the storm can no longer support the debris, and it will fall to the ground in an area where there is no sign of bad weather!

There have even been reports of frozen fish falling from the sky! In those cases, the tornado passed over a pond and picked up its contents, including the fish. The water and fish were lifted way up into the atmosphere, to a height where the air can be as cold as -90 degrees Fahrenheit (F)/-68 degrees Celsius (C). The fish became encased in ice balls, and then dropped from the sky. Once a fish went right through the windshield of an automobile! It was because of this extreme weather phenomena that I originally wanted to name this book *Did You Know That Fish Could Fly . . . and Other Acts of Cod.*

More tornadoes occur in the United States than in any other country on Earth. On average, nearly 1,000 tornadoes are reported each year. What actually causes a tornado to drop from a thunderstorm still remains unknown. Even when all the ingredients for a tornado are present, the storm may never form. This is a great mystery to the scientists and meteorologists who study tornadoes.

How Are Tornadoes Born?

To understand how a tornado works, we must first understand where it comes from. Tornadoes are born from thunderstorms. Thunderstorms form in unstable air when there is warm air at the ground and cold air aloft. Due to this temperature profile, most thunderstorms occur in spring and summer, rather than in fall and winter. In spring, the

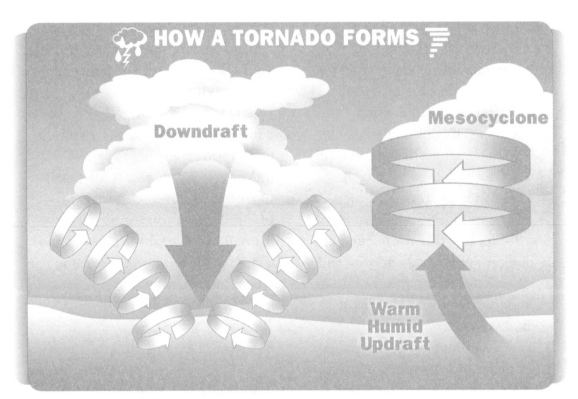

sun warms the air at ground level, which rises into the cold winter air that still remains high above in the atmosphere at that time of year. This mix of warm and cold can cause violent thunderstorms that create not only tornadoes, but also destructive straight-line winds, damaging hail, and extensive flooding from heavy rains. In fall, the air at ground level is also warmed, but it rises into the warm summer air that remains aloft, so thunderstorms, and tornadoes, form less often.

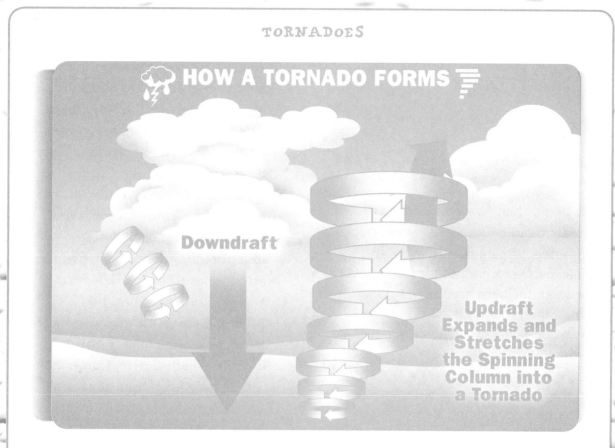

HOW A TORNADO FORMS

Downdraft

Updraft Expands and Stretches the Spinning Column into a Tornado

The Life of a Thunderstorm

Updrafts—warm, humid air rises from the ground (**Towering Cumulus Stage**).

As the air cools to its dew point, it forms a cloud.

Ice crystals or water drops grow big enough to overcome the updraft, they begin falling, dragging down the air (**Mature Stage**).

The falling precipitation and air being dragged down form downdrafts.

Updrafts continue feeding warm, humid air into the storm. Existence of both updrafts and downdrafts make this the storm's most violent stage.

Downdrafts grow, choking off updrafts (**Dissipating Stage**); with its supply of humid air cut, the storm begins dying and rain tapers off.

What Are the Best Conditions for a Tornado?

Extreme thunderstorms, ones that create deadly tornadoes, have special ingredients. The most deadly and destructive tornadoes form from *super cells*—which are rotating thunderstorms with a well-defined radar circulation called a *mesocyclone* (which we will discuss later). This type of storm is rare and only occurs in the United States. Characteristics of tornado-producing storms include:

- ❉ Unstable air that's forced upward
- ❉ An upper-air disturbance in the flow
- ❉ A fresh supply of warm, humid air flowing near the ground with high-altitude cold air flowing in
- ❉ Wind speeds that increase with altitude, like the jet stream. This interacts with the updrafts, promoting rotation in the storm. Upper-level winds promote and sustain the life of the storm, making it, in most cases, even stronger and thus a super storm.
- ❉ Downbursts that can be invisible clean air, or lashing or sideways rains. Their abrupt change in wind direction poses a threat to airplanes that are landing and taking off. Doppler radar at airports detects and warns pilots of dangerous downbursts.

Colored Tornadoes, Rope Tornadoes, and Other Varietals

Most tornadoes are dark because of the debris, dust, and dirt the storm has sucked up from the ground. Tornadoes can be many colors. They can be red from red dirt. Tornadoes can be white from water or from picking up snow in mountainous areas.

Tornadoes tend to look darkest to people who are on the east side of the storm. The tornado is often silhouetted in front of the brighter skies to the west of the thunderstorm. If there is heavy rain behind the tornado, it may look dark gray, blue, or even white—depending on where most of the daylight is coming from. Tornadoes wrapped in rain may exhibit varieties of gray shades on gray.

There are slang terms for tornadoes like "a wedge tornado" or "a rope tornado," which are basically used by tornado spotters to describe a tornado's shape and appearance. This does not by any means, however, say anything certain about a tornado's strength! Wedge tornadoes simply appear as wide as they are tall. Rope tornadoes are very narrow and often snakelike in appearance.

A Few More Tornado Facts

Nearly 60 percent of tornadoes occur between noon and sunset. This is the time when the sun most heats the atmosphere, creating unstable conditions. The jet stream also plays an important role as it enhances super-storm cell development.

Some tornadoes can have wind speeds of up to 300 mph. A small storm could be as slow as 50 mph and last a few minutes. A large monster can last for several hours and travel as far as 250 miles.

On average, sixty people are killed by tornadoes each year. Boards, roof shingles, glass, stones, and bricks turn into missiles and cause most tornado-related deaths.

There is a major difference between a tornado and what's called a "funnel cloud." In a tornado, the damaging circulation is *on the ground*—whether or not the cloud is. A true funnel cloud rotates, but has no ground contact. However, a funnel cloud is still dangerous and you should still avoid it! Some funnels may never touch the ground. As the funnel descends, the rotation speed increases. It becomes a tornado when it touches the ground and dramatically increases in speed and power as it feeds on the warmer surface air. If you see one, you should report it to either the local police, fire, or sheriff's department, as well as your local office of the National Weather Service.

Where Is Tornado Alley?

Even though we know most tornadoes occur during the spring and summer, there is no "tornado season" (though there is a hurricane season). Still, there are certain

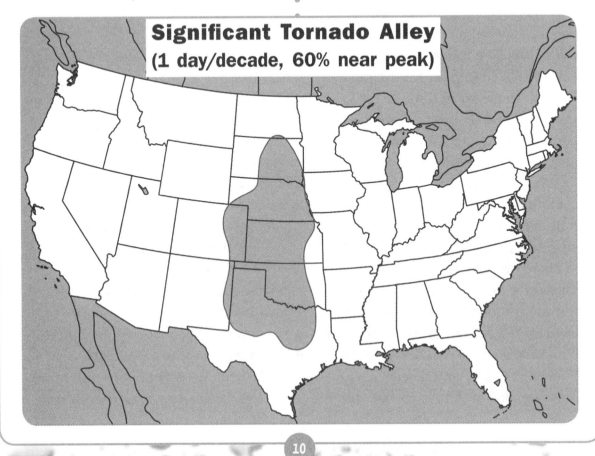

Significant Tornado Alley
(1 day/decade, 60% near peak)

times and areas where tornadoes are most likely to occur. From Texas to Oklahoma, through Arkansas to Illinois, through Nebraska to the Dakotas is the area that is called *tornado alley*, where most tornadoes are likely to occur during any given year. Looking at the map on page 10, however, you can see that if you live anywhere from South Dakota to most of Texas, from eastern Colorado to the eastern edges of the Midwest, you have a greater chance of experiencing a tornado than if you live in the Northeast, or mid-Atlantic, or on the Pacific coast. It's all but guaranteed that if you live in Oklahoma or Texas you will experience at least one tornado every one or two years.

Tornado Swarms

It is the rarest of storm types, but the super cell is the most dangerous because of the extreme weather it can generate. Since super cells can travel as far as 300 miles, multiple numbers of tornadoes can be created. This doesn't always occur, but when it does, these are called "swarms" of tornadoes. Super cells can be regenerated over a period of days along a cold front or what is called a *squall line* (a moving line of severe weather across a major portion of the country).

Ten Greatest Tornado Swarms

NUMBER OF TORNADOES	DATE	DEATHS
148	April 3–4, 1974	315
111	September 19–23, 1967	5
99	May 26–27, 1973	22
95	November 21–23, 1992	26
94	May 4–5, 2003	37
85	May 22–23, 2004	1
80	February 5–6, 2008	60
80	May 18–19, 1995	4
78	May 3–4, 1999	46
70	May 11–12, 1982	2
67	April 26–27, 1994	3

TOP TEN: U.S. CITIES MOST AT RISK FOR TORNADOES

1. Oklahoma City, Oklahoma
2. Dallas–Ft. Worth, Texas
3. Lubbock, Texas
4. Kansas City, Missouri
5. Indianapolis, Indiana
6. St. Louis, Missouri
7. Jackson, Mississippi, and Birmingham, Alabama
8. Little Rock, Arkansas
9. Omaha, Nebraska
10. Chicago, Illinois

Most Tornado-Prone Areas in the United States

Highest Absolute Number of Tornado Occurrences

1. Texas
2. Oklahoma
3. Florida

Highest Absolute Number of Killer Tornado Occurrences

1. Texas
2. Oklahoma
3. Arkansas

Highest Absolute Number of Tornado Fatalities

1. Texas
2. Mississippi
3. Alabama

Most Tornadoes in Any Month

The record for the most tornadoes in any month (since modern tornado record keeping began in 1950) was set in April 2011 with 875 tornadoes. This easily broke the old mark of 543, set in May 2003.

Most Tornadoes in Any Month Since 1950

1. April 2011   875
2. May 2003   543
3. June 1992   399
4. May 1995   391
5. June 1998   376
6. May 1991   335
7. May 1982   329
8. June 1990   329
9. June 1993   313
10. May 1998   310

TEN DEADLIEST SINGLE TORNADOES

NOAA ONLY STARTED tracking tornado fatalities in 1950. Prior to 1950, information about tornado fatalities was gathered by an independent research group, The Tornado Project. Data in this table is drawn from both NOAA and The Tornado Project.

DEATHS	INJURED	LOCATION	DATE	LENGTH MI.	WIDTH YDS.
695	2027	MO, IL, IN	March 18, 1925	219	1200
317	109	Natchez, MS	May 7, 1840	35	1000
255	1000	St. Louis, MO	May 27, 1896	12	800
216	700	Tupelo, MS	April 5, 1936	15	1000
203	1600	Gainesville, GA	April 6, 1936	7	400
181	970	Woodward, OK	April 9, 1947	170	1500
151	1000+	Joplin, MO	May 22, 2011	6	750
143	770	Amite, LA– Purvis, MS	April 24, 1908	135	1000
117	200	New Richmond, WI	June 12, 1899	30	300
115	115	Flint, MI	June 8, 1953	27	800

Biggest Tornado Ever!

The biggest known tornado is the Hallam, Nebraska, F4 tornado of May 22, 2004. Its peak width was nearly two and a half miles. This is probably close to the maximum size for tornadoes.

Strongest Tornado Ever!

We don't know how fast winds can go inside a tornado. Tornado wind speeds have only been directly recorded in weaker storms, because strong and violent tornadoes destroy weather instruments. Mobile Doppler radars (which we will discuss later), such as the Oklahoma University "Doppler on Wheels," have remotely sensed tornado wind speeds above ground level as high as about 302 mph (on May 3, 1999, near Bridge Creek, Oklahoma; that tornado caused F5 damage—this was before the introduction of the EF scale). These are the highest winds ever found on the Earth's surface, even faster than hurricane winds. But ground-level wind speeds in the most violent tornadoes have never been directly measured.

The Enhanced Fujita Damage Scale

The Enhanced Fujita Scale, or EF Scale, is the scale for rating the strength of tornadoes in the United States, estimated by the damage they cause. The original "F" scale was invented in 1971 by University of Chicago physicist Theodore Fujita, the first and foremost tornado scientist.

The new, enhanced Fujita (EF) scale went into operation on February 1, 2007. The scale was revised to reflect current, better examinations of tornado damage surveys, and to align wind speeds more closely with associated storm damage. The new scale takes into account more types of structures as well as vegetation, expands degrees of damage, and better accounts for variables such as the differences in construction of buildings and structures.

The EF scale is not intended to assess wind speed as much as it is to derive what the wind speeds were in a particular tornado as determined by the type of damage that was left behind by the storm. The new scale takes into account quality of construction and standardizes different kinds of structures. The wind speeds on the original scale were deemed too high by meteorologists and engineers, and engineering studies indicated that slower winds than initially estimated caused the respective degrees of damage.

The following graphic shows the damage assessment from the Enhanced Fujita Scale and what the corresponding tornado might look like. Images are courtesy of the National Severe Storms Lab.

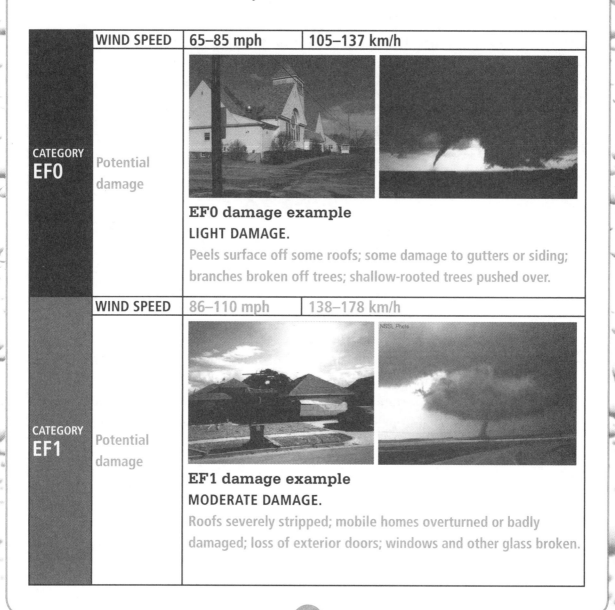

CATEGORY EF0	WIND SPEED	65–85 mph	105–137 km/h

EF0 damage example
LIGHT DAMAGE.
Peels surface off some roofs; some damage to gutters or siding; branches broken off trees; shallow-rooted trees pushed over.

CATEGORY EF1	WIND SPEED	86–110 mph	138–178 km/h

EF1 damage example
MODERATE DAMAGE.
Roofs severely stripped; mobile homes overturned or badly damaged; loss of exterior doors; windows and other glass broken.

		WIND SPEED	111–135 mph	179–218 km/h
CATEGORY EF2	Potential damage			

EF2 damage example
CONSIDERABLE DAMAGE.
Roofs torn off well-constructed houses; foundations of frame homes shifted; mobile homes completely destroyed; large trees snapped or uprooted; light-object missiles generated; cars lifted off ground.

		WIND SPEED	136–165 mph	219–266 km/h
CATEGORY EF3	Potential damage			

EF3 damage example
SEVERE DAMAGE.
Entire stories of well-constructed houses destroyed; severe damage to large buildings such as shopping malls; trains overturned; trees debarked; heavy cars lifted off the ground and thrown; structures with weak foundations blown away some distance.

	WIND SPEED	166–200 mph	267–322 km/h
CATEGORY **EF4**	Potential damage	EF4 damage example **DEVASTATING DAMAGE.** Well-constructed houses and whole frame houses completely leveled; cars thrown and refrigerator-sized missiles generated.	
	WIND SPEED	>200 mph	>322 km/h
CATEGORY **EF5**	Potential damage	EF5 damage example **INCREDIBLE DAMAGE.** Strong frame houses leveled off foundations and swept away; automobile-sized missiles fly through the air in excess of 100m (109 yd); high-rise buildings have significant structural deformation; incredible phenomena will occur. An example of this took place on May 23, 2011, when an EF5 tornado destroyed half of Joplin, Missouri, cutting a 6-mile-wide path through the city.	

What Is a Derecho?

Thunderstorms not only destroy lives and property by spawning tornadoes, they contain another type of wind that can be just as destructive. A prolonged windstorm that produces straight-line winds rather than or in addition to a tornado is called a *derecho*. Derecho (pronounced deh-RAY-cho) is the Spanish word for

"direct" or "straight ahead" and describes the winds that can be produced by thunderstorms. Straight-line winds that come from a thunderstorm can be as fast as 100 miles per hour.

Super cell: King of Thunderstorms

Common thunderstorms are born and rain themselves out within a very short period of time, say an hour or less. Super cells are the most dangerous because they can develop the strongest tornadoes. They can travel more than 300 miles across

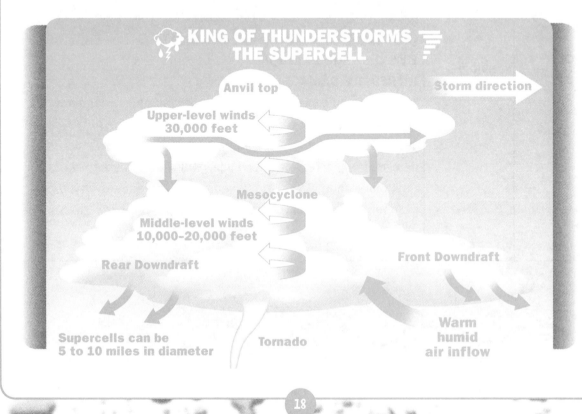

KING OF THUNDERSTORMS THE SUPERCELL

Anvil top

Storm direction

Upper-level winds 30,000 feet

Mesocyclone

Middle-level winds 10,000–20,000 feet

Front Downdraft

Rear Downdraft

Supercells can be 5 to 10 miles in diameter

Tornado

Warm humid air inflow

the country as well and cause heavy, flooding rain; large, damaging hail; and straight-line (or derecho) winds in excess of 100 mph. Super cells need humid, unstable air, and some lifting force (like the jet stream) to move the air upward. Super cells can last as long as 5 to 8 hours.

A rotating column of rising air, called a *mesocyclone*, is the key to the long life of a super cell. It gathers in the warm, humid air near the ground and mixes it with the cool, dry air from above. The mesocyclone supplies the spin that strong tornadoes require.

Most Damaging Tornadoes (F5 and EF5) in the U.S. since 1950

This is a list of tornadoes since 1950 which the National Weather Service has rated F5 (before 2007) or EF5 (2007 on—the most intense damage category on the Fujita and Enhanced Fujita damage scales. The tornadoes are numbered in the order they happened since 1950; so the numbers run from the bottom up.

MOST DAMAGING TORNADOES IN U.S. SINCE 1950

NUMBER	DATE	LOCATION
58	May 24, 2011	El Reno/Piedmont, OK
57	May 22, 2011	Joplin, MO
56	April 27, 2011	Rainsville/Sylvania, AL
55	April 27, 2011	Preston, MS
54	April 27, 2011	Hackleburg/Phil Campbell, AL
53	April 27, 2011	Smithville, MS
52	May 25, 2008	Parkersburg, IA
51	May 4, 2007	Greensburg, KS
50	May 3, 1999	Bridge Creek/Moore, OK
49	April 16, 1998	Waynesboro, TN
48	April 8, 1998	Oak Grove/Pleasant Grove, AL
47	May 27, 1997	Jarrell, TX
46	July 18, 1996	Oakfield, WI
45	June 16, 1992	Chandler, MN
44	April 26, 1991	Andover, KS
43	August 28, 1990	Plainfield, IL
42	March 13, 1990	Goessel, KS
41	March 13, 1990	Hesston, KS
40	May 31, 1985	Niles, OH
39	June 7, 1984	Barneveld, WI
38	April 2, 1982	Broken Bow, OK
37	April 4, 1977	Birmingham, AL
36	June 13, 1976	Jordan, IA
35	April 19, 1976	Brownwood, TX
34	March 26, 1976	Spiro, OK
33	April 3, 1974	Guin, AL
32	April 3, 1974	Tanner, AL

NUMBER	DATE	LOCATION
31	April 3, 1974	Mt. Hope, AL
30	April 3, 1974	Sayler Park, OH
29	April 3, 1974	Brandenburg, KY
28	April 3, 1974	Xenia, OH
27	April 3, 1974	Daisy Hill, IN
26	May 6, 1973	Valley Mills, TX
25	February 21, 1971	Delhi, LA
24	May 11, 1970	Lubbock, TX
23	June 13, 1968	Tracy, MN
22	May 15, 1968	Maynard, IA
21	May 15, 1968	Charles City, IA
20	April 23, 1968	Gallipolis, OH
19	October 14, 1966	Belmond, IA
18	June 8, 1966	Topeka, KS
17	March 3, 1966	Jackson, MS
16	May 8, 1965	Gregory, SD
15	May 5, 1964	Bradshaw, NE
14	April 3, 1964	Wichita Falls, TX
13	May 5, 1960	Prague, OK
12	June 4, 1958	Menomonie, WI
11	December 18, 1957	Murphysboro, IL
10	June 20, 1957	Fargo, ND
9	May 20, 1957	Ruskin Heights, MO
8	April 3, 1956	Grand Rapids, MI
7	May 25, 1955	Udall, KS
6	May 25, 1955	Blackwell, OK
5	December 5, 1953	Vicksburg, MS
4	June 27, 1953	Adair, IA
3	June 8, 1953	Flint, MI
2	May 29, 1953	Ft. Rice, ND
1	May 11, 1953	Waco, TX

THE 17 DEADLIEST DAYS IN U.S. TORNADO HISTORY

(Since 1950)

Courtesy Storm Prediction Center; Compiled by Greg Carbin, Roger Edwards, and Joe Schaefer, SPC

Please note that data from 2011 is incomplete.

RANK	BEGINNING DATE	DEATHS
1	May 22, 2011	695
2	April 27, 2011	313
3	April 3, 1974	310
4	April 11, 1965	260
5	March 21, 1952	205
6	June 8, 1953	142
7	May 11, 1953	127
8	February 21, 1971	121
9	May 25, 1955	102
10	June 9, 1953	90
11	May 31, 1985	76
12	May 15, 1968	72
13(tie)	March 3, 1966	58
13(tie)	April 21, 1967	58
15(tie)	April 10, 1979	57
15(tie)	March 28, 1984	57
15(tie)	February 5, 2008	57

Waterspout: Cousin to the Tornado

A waterspout is a tornado over water. Waterspouts are common along the southeast U.S. coast—especially off southern Florida and the Keys—but they have been seen as far north as New York City, over the Great Lakes, and even off the coast of California. In one season, as many as 390 waterspouts were observed within 50 miles of the

Florida Keys, making them far more prevalent than previously thought.

Waterspouts occur over seas, bays, and lakes worldwide. Although waterspouts are tornadoes, they don't officially count in tornado records unless they hit land. Waterspouts commonly come from rapidly growing cumulus clouds that have not and often do not become thunderstorms. Waterspouts are smaller and weaker than the most intense Great Plains tornadoes, but still can be quite dangerous. They can cause the same type of damage as an EF0 or an EF1. Waterspouts can overturn small boats, damage ships, do significant damage when hitting land, and kill people.

What Is the Difference Between a Tornado Watch and a Tornado Warning?

A tornado watch means that approaching weather *may* produce a tornado. In a tornado watch, you need to be alert to the fact that the weather conditions are favorable for the formation of tornadoes. You need to be prepared to go to a safe shelter or other place of safety if tornadoes do happen or if a warning is issued. This is the time to turn on local TV or radio to get the latest information. You should also make sure your friends and family are aware of the potential for tornadoes in the area.

URGENT—IMMEDIATE BROADCAST REQUESTED
TORNADO WATCH NUMBER 600
NWS STORM PREDICTION CENTER NORMAN OK
1030 PM EDT WED AUG 15 2007

THE NWS STORM PREDICTION CENTER HAS ISSUED A
TORNADO WATCH FOR PORTIONS OF
    NORTHERN INDIANA
    NORTHWEST OHIO
    LAKE MICHIGAN

EFFECTIVE THIS WEDNESDAY NIGHT AND THURSDAY MORNING FROM 1030 PM UNTIL 400 AM
EDT.

TORNADOES . . . HAIL TO 1 INCH IN DIAMETER . . . THUNDERSTORM WIND GUSTS TO 70 MPH . . .
AND DANGEROUS LIGHTNING ARE POSSIBLE IN THESE AREAS.

THE TORNADO WATCH AREA IS APPROXIMATELY ALONG AND 40 STATUTE MILES NORTH
AND SOUTH OF A LINE FROM 20 MILES SOUTH SOUTHWEST OF VALPARAISO INDIANA TO 65
MILES EAST OF FORT WAYNE INDIANA. FOR A COMPLETE DEPICTION OF THE WATCH SEE THE
ASSOCIATED WATCH OUTLINE UPDATE (WOUS64 KWNS WOU0).

REMEMBER . . . A TORNADO WATCH MEANS CONDITIONS ARE FAVORABLE FOR TORNADOES
AND SEVERE THUNDERSTORMS IN AND CLOSE TO THE WATCH AREA. PERSONS IN THESE AREAS
SHOULD BE ON THE LOOKOUT FOR THREATENING WEATHER CONDITIONS AND LISTEN FOR
LATER STATEMENTS AND POSSIBLE WARNINGS.

DISCUSSION . . . SMALL MCS OVER NW IND HAS FORMED IN THE PAST 90 MINUTES ON WRN
SIDE OF COLD POOL/MCV ASSOCIATED WITH EARLIER CONVECTIVE SYSTEM. THE MCS SHOULD
REMAIN STRONG THROUGH EARLY THURSDAY AND TRACK ESE INTO OH. A Super cell NOW
PRESENT ON WRN SIDE OF SYSTEM WILL POSE A THREAT FOR ISOLATED TORNADOES . . . IN
ADDITION TO DAMAGING WET MICROBURSTS/ MARGINALLY SVR HAIL . . . GIVEN HI PWS AND
LOW LEVEL WIND FIELD WITH CONSIDERABLE DEGREE OF SPEED/DIRECTIONAL SHEAR. WIND
PROFILES MAY ALSO SUPPORT BACK-BUILDING DEVELOPMENT ON WRN SIDE OF MCS . . . WITH
ASSOCIATED LOCALLY HEAVY RAIN POSSIBLE INTO FAR NE IL/NRN IND IN WAKE OF Super cell.

AVIATION . . . TORNADOES AND A FEW SEVERE THUNDERSTORMS WITH HAIL SURFACE AND
ALOFT TO 1 INCH. EXTREME TURBULENCE AND SURFACE WIND GUSTS TO 60 KNOTS. A FEW
CUMULONIMBI WITH MAXIMUM TOPS TO 550. MEAN STORM MOTION VECTOR 30030.

. . . CORFIDI*

Once the outline of a watch area is defined by the NWS Storm Prediction Center, a list of counties within the watch area is posted to make sure residents and travelers understand exactly which counties are possibly

*This is the National Weather Service forecaster who issued the watch.

in the path of a future tornado. These watch areas are shown on television by a meteorologist or weathercaster, and the counties are named in a special weather bulletin on radio and television. Many television broadcast or cable channels will scroll the names of the counties across the TV screen in what is called a *crawl*.

Example of a Watch County Breakdown

```
WOUS64 KWNS 160227
WOU0


BULLETIN—IMMEDIATE BROADCAST REQUESTED
TORNADO WATCH OUTLINE UPDATE FOR WT 600
NWS STORM PREDICTION CENTER NORMAN OK
1030 PM EDT WED AUG 15 2007

TORNADO WATCH 600 IS IN EFFECT UNTIL 400 AM EDT FOR THE FOLLOWING LOCATIONS

INC001-003-009-017-033-039-049-053-069-075-085-087-091-099-103-113-131-141-149-151-169-179-
181-183-160800-/O.NEW.KWNS.TO.A.0600.070816T0230Z-070816T0800Z/

IN
INDIANA COUNTIES INCLUDED ARE

ADAMS      ALLEN      BLACKFORD
CASS       DE KALB    ELKHART
FULTON     GRANT      HUNTINGTON
JAY        KOSCIUSKO  LAGRANGE
LA PORTE   MARSHALL   MIAMI
NOBLE      PULASKI    ST. JOSEPH
STARKE     STEUBEN    WABASH
WELLS      WHITE      WHITLEY


OHC003-039-051-069-125-137-161-171-160800-/O.NEW.KWNS.TO.A.0600.070816T0230Z-
070816T0800Z/

OH
OHIO COUNTIES INCLUDED ARE

ALLEN      DEFIANCE   FULTON
HENRY      PAULDING   PUTNAM
VAN WERT   WILLIAMS


LMZ046-160800-/O.NEW.KWNS.TO.A.0600.070816T0230Z-070816T0800Z/
CW
ADJACENT COASTAL WATERS INCLUDED ARE

MICHIGAN CITY IN TO NEW BUFFALO MI
```

Tornado Warning

A tornado warning is issued when a hook echo is indicated on weather radar. A hook echo is produced when rain, hail, or debris is wrapped around a super cell, indicating that the hook echo that has been sighted could potentially drop down to the ground and become a tornado.

A tornado warning is also issued when an official weather spotter (someone who is trained to detect a tornado with the human eye) sees a funnel cloud and alerts local authorities such as police, sheriff, fire department, or the local National Weather Service office. It can take only a few moments between a funnel cloud being sighted on radar and a tornado touching down. By the time a warning is heard on radio or seen on television, the tornado may already be on the ground.

It's important to know the details and find out if your county is in the watch area. Have a plan and be ready to act if and when a tornado warning is issued.

How to Save Yourself If You Are Ever Caught in a Tornado

Know the signs of a tornado: Weather forecasting science is not perfect and some tornadoes do occur without a tornado warning. There is no substitute for staying alert to the sky. Besides an obviously visible tornado, here are some things to look and listen for:

Strong, persistent rotation in the cloud base.

Whirling dust or debris on the ground under a cloud base—tornadoes sometimes have no funnel!

Hail or heavy rain followed by either dead calm or a fast, intense wind shift. Many tornadoes are wrapped in heavy precipitation and can't be seen.

Day or night: Loud, continuous roar or rumble that doesn't fade in a few seconds like thunder.

Night: Small, bright, blue-green to white flashes at ground level near a thunderstorm (as opposed to silvery lightning up in the clouds). These mean that power lines are being snapped by a very strong wind, maybe a tornado.

Night: Persistent lowering from the cloud base, illuminated or silhouetted by lightning—especially if it is on the ground or there is a blue-green to white power flash underneath.

HOW TO SAVE YOURSELF FROM A TORNADO

Roofs that aren't attached well can be ripped off by 60 mph winds

▶ WHAT TO DO DURING A TORNADO

In a house with a basement:
Avoid windows. Get in the basement and under some kind of sturdy protection like a heavy table or workbench, or cover yourself with a mattress or sleeping bag. Know where very heavy objects rest on the floor above (like pianos, refrigerators, or waterbeds) and do not go under them. They may fall through a weakened floor and crush you.

In a house with no basement, a dorm, or an apartment: Avoid windows. Go to the lowest floor; into a small, windowless chamber like a bathroom or closet; under a stairwell; or into an interior hallway with no windows. Crouch as low as possible to the floor, facing down, and cover your head with your hands. A bathtub may offer partial protection. Even in an interior room, you should cover yourself with some sort of thick padding, like a mattress or blankets, to protect yourself against falling debris in case the roof or ceiling fails. Do not waste time opening windows—it won't protect your home from damage and if a tornado hits your building it's likely to blow out the windows anyway.

In an office building, a hospital, a nursing home, or a skyscraper:
Go directly to an enclosed, windowless area in the center of the building. Crouch down and cover your head. Interior stairwells are usually good places to take shelter. If the stairs are not crowded, move quickly to a lower level. Stay out of the elevators; you could be trapped in them if the power is lost.

In a mobile home: Get out! Even if your home is tied down, you are probably safer outside, even if the only alternative is to seek shelter out in the open. Most tornadoes can destroy even tied-down mobile homes, and it is best not to play the low odds that yours will make it. If your community has a tornado shelter, go there fast. If there is a sturdy permanent building within easy running distance, seek shelter there. Otherwise, lie flat on low ground away from your home, protecting your head. If possible, use open ground away from trees and cars, which can be blown onto you.

At school: Follow the drill! Go to the interior hall or room in an orderly way, as you are told. Crouch low, head down, and protect the back of your head with your arms. Stay away from windows and large open rooms like gyms and auditoriums.

In a car or truck: Vehicles are extremely dangerous in a tornado. If the tornado is visible, far away, and the traffic is light, you may be able to drive out of its path by moving at right angles to the tornado. Otherwise, park the car as quickly and safely as possible—out of the traffic lanes. (It's safer to get the car out of any mud later, if necessary, than to cause a crash by stopping in the roadway.) Get out and seek shelter in a sturdy building. If you are in open country, run to low ground away from any cars. Lie flat and facedown, protecting the back of your head with your arms. Avoid seeking shelter under bridges, which can create deadly traffic hazards while offering little protection against flying debris.

In the open, out of doors: If possible, seek shelter in a sturdy building nearby. If not, lie flat and facedown on low ground, protecting the back of your head with your arms. Get as far away from trees and cars as you can; they may be blown onto you.

In a shopping mall or a large store: Do not panic. Stay aware of crowds. Move as quickly as

possible to an interior bathroom, storage room, or other small enclosed area, away from windows. Crouch facedown and protect your head with your arms.

In a theater or other public building: Do not panic. If possible, move quickly and in an orderly fashion to an interior bathroom or hallway, away from windows. Crouch facedown and protect your head with your arms. If there is no time to do that, get under the seats or pews, protecting your head with your arms or hands.

▶ **WHAT TO DO AFTER THE TORNADO**

Keep your family together and wait for emergency personnel to arrive. If you can, render aid to those who are injured. Stay away from power lines and puddles with wires in them; they may still be carrying electricity. Watch your step to avoid broken glass, nails, or other sharp objects. Stay out of any heavily damaged houses or buildings; they could collapse at any time. Do not use matches or lighters, in case there are leaking natural gas pipes or fuel tanks nearby. Remain calm and alert, and listen for information and instructions from emergency crews or local officials.

Tornado Chasers— Are They Crazy?

Want to feel your heart pounding in your chest? Want to feel the real-life fright of your life? You're excited yet anxious, nervous and scared, trying to keep your composure. Who are you? You're a *tornado chaser* experiencing a very real once-in-a-lifetime thrill ride. I have done it personally and I can tell you, there is nothing scarier than standing right in front of an approaching tornado spinning at 250 mph.

I'm in western Oklahoma, it's late in the day. I'm with a crew of chasers equipped with cameras and a portable Doppler radar, driving right into the teeth of a nasty super cell, into the area known as the "bear's cage." It's the area between the main updraft of the storm and the hail. Pritt J. Vesilind, who chased

tornadoes for *National Geographic,* put it this way: "It's aptly called the bear's cage, because chasing tornadoes is like hunting grizzlies— you want to get close, but not on the same side of the river. Sometimes you get the bear; sometimes the bear gets you."

The sky is pea green and black but everything is calm as we approach the super cell. When we enter the mammoth storm, we're immediately hit with a ripping gust of straight-line winds of 60 mph. Rain is pouring down as if it was being poured out of a pitcher onto our van. We can't see a thing. Brilliant lightning is zapping and snaking all around, sounding like cannons.

It wasn't a good idea to drive head-on into the storm's fury, but we were on the only road in the desolation of this part of western Oklahoma. Emergency vehicles, flashing red lights, sheriff's deputies, storms chasers, and spotters are everywhere.

The road takes us slightly to the storm's right, where we are blasted with hail the size of golf balls, and some larger! The van's windshield cracks from the force of the hail. As we fearfully press on, outside we can see the wall cloud where the tornadoes would be found. Inside, the crew is looking at Doppler radar and the instruments, getting a fix on the super cell's path.

We see beautiful mammatus clouds overhead and the sky begins to take on a reddish hue in the light of the setting sun. The rain and hail end. The crew stops to set up the camera outside. The world looks eerie and very frightening. The Doppler radar shows a hook echo. Our excitement and anticipation grow. We hope to see this awesome, beautiful freak of nature drop from the sky. Dark clouds billow across an open field in front of us right before we're hit with another round of hail. In the distance we can see a vortex spinning at the surface, picking up dust and dirt as the tornado snakes down to meet it.

I jump in front of the camera to describe what I'm seeing; my heart is pounding and I'm nearly out of breath. Barely able to contain my composure, I do a play-by-play of the tornado as it spins up debris: soil, plants, and eventually some power lines. As the storm crosses the road going away from us, it climbs back into the cloud as quickly as it had descended. Fortunately, no homes were destroyed and no one was hurt.

The crew was great, courageous, and brave. I was very happy to have witnessed this powerful, awesome form of extreme weather and to be heading home safe and sound.

Weather Myths Solved!

One of the most frequent questions I get asked when I speak to students is "Will opening windows to equalize the air pressure save my house from destruction by a tornado?"

I've always wondered who originally thought of such an idea. Most likely it was born of the desire to do something, anything, to make the tornado less harmful or to somehow ward it off. Well, let me tell you, raising a window is certainly not going to render an EF5 tornado harmless! In reality, this is a dangerous and useless waste of time. Instead of opening windows, you should be getting to a place of safety. Raising a window will do nothing to stop one of the most violent forces on the planet.

Since I am a meteorologist in New York City, one of the largest cities in America, kids often say to me, "Tornadoes never hit big cities." Well, that was disproved in the spring of 2007 when a funnel cloud was sighted on Doppler radar over Staten Island, New York. It passed over New York Harbor and touched down in Brooklyn, New York, as an EF1. The tornado uprooted trees, damaged roofs, and blew over fences. The last time that happened was 100 years earlier. Tornadoes do not form in big cities as often as they do in tornado alley, but they're not unknown in metropolitan areas. The Dallas–Ft. Worth area in Texas has been hit with tornadoes. Oklahoma City is often rife with tornadoes. St. Louis, Kansas City, Indianapolis, Omaha, Chicago, and Detroit have all experienced tornadoes right in town or in their suburbs! The incorrect idea that one's town is protected is due to short memory, the rarity of tornadoes, and wishful thinking!

While chasing tornadoes in Oklahoma, I thought to myself, "If we need to seek safety from an approaching tornado, would a highway overpass be a safe place?" Well, common sense should dictate that anytime you find yourself aboveground in the path of a tornado, either deliberately or by coincidence, you are in harm's way. Every year, dozens of drivers pull off highways in the face of an oncoming tornado and run under overpasses. They also block the road near the overpasses, putting other motorists in extreme danger. On May 4, 1999, this myth was put to rest when a woman and her child climbed underneath an overpass

An EF-2 tornado forms over the University of Alabama campus in Huntsville, Alabama, on January 21, 2010.

with several other people. The intense winds grasped the woman and, unfortunately, carried her half a mile to her death. Her child was only slightly injured. It's too bad this myth could not be dispelled before someone was killed.

When driving home from college once on a rural road, I was flagged down by the highway patrol. They were making everyone get out of their cars and lie in a roadside ditch because a tornado was coming right at us. I could see the funnel cloud as it passed over us in the dim sunset light. I had never been so happy to be lying in a rain-soaked, muddy ditch before! Since we were lower than the surface of the land around us, we survived unhurt.

Those who live in tornado alley always hear "the southwest corner of a basement is the safest location during passage of a tornado." People often say this because we know that tornadoes generally move along a cold front or squall line from southwest to northeast. But is it really true? In 1996, Professor Joseph Eagleman from the University of Kansas proved that this could be a deadly choice. Eagleman found that actually the southwest part of the basement was the worst place to be because of the way houses moved during a tornado. In a tornado, a home can be shifted off its foundation. If it collapses, it can sometimes crush people who sought shelter in the basement. As a general rule, basements are a safe place during a tornado, but sometimes even a basement is not safe.

Tornado Oddities

The Great Bend, Kansas, tornado of November 1915, is the tornado that seems to have the greatest number of oddities associated with it. To begin with, it was an unusual time of year—in fact, it is the latest in the year that a violent tornado has ever struck the state of Kansas. The funnel began its late-evening journey 5 miles southwest of Larned, 16 miles southwest of Great Bend. Because it was nearly dark, the tornado was visible only occasionally, during flashes of lightning. The oddities began southwest of Pawnee Rock, where a farm was leveled to the ground and two people were killed. From a short distance away, one could not tell that a farmstead had ever existed there. Five horses were the only survivors. They were carried a quarter-mile away from the barn and found, completely unhurt and hitched to the same rail.

At the edge of Great Bend, the Charles Hammond house was unroofed. The family was completely unaware of the damage until they went outside to see what had happened to a neighbor's home. The south wall of Grant Jones's store was blown down, but shelves and canned goods that stood against the wall were unmoved. The Riverside Steam Laundry, built of stone and cement block, was reduced to a fragment of upright wall, yet two nearby wooden shacks seemed almost untouched.

At the Moses Clay ranch, on the east edge of town, 1,000 sheep were killed, the most ever killed by a single tornado. A cancelled check from Great Bend was found in a cornfield, one mile outside of Palmyra, Nebraska . . . 305 miles to the northeast, the longest known distance that debris has ever been carried. Receipts, checks, photographs, ledger sheets, money, clothing, shingles, and fragments of books rained down on almost every farm north and west of Glasco, 80 miles to the northeast of Great Bend.

A necktie rack with ten ties still attached was carried 40 miles. A four-page letter from a swain to his fair damsel was carried 70 miles. A flour sack from the Walnut Creek Mill was found 110 miles to the northeast, perhaps the longest distance ever recorded for an object weighing more than one pound. Up to 45,000 migrating ducks were reported killed at Cheyenne Bottoms. Dead ducks fell from the sky 40 miles northeast of that migratory bird refuge.

In Great Bend, an iron water hydrant was found full of splinters. Mail was lifted from the railroad depot and scattered for miles to the northeast. Some of it was returned to Great Bend, but some was sent on from where it had been found . . . one of the earliest forms of airmail! Farmers living 2 miles from town were unaware of the tragedy and were dumbfounded when they visited town the next day and beheld the tragic spectacle. Over 20,000 visitors viewed the wreckage the following Sunday.

Things that seemed impossible were discovered for days after the storm. An iron jug was blown inside out. A rooster was blown into a jug, with only its head sticking out of the neck of the container!

Fish Falling from the Sky!

History mentions many instances of things (other than rain, snow, sleet, hail, or other usual forms of precipitation) falling from the sky. I have personally seen it happen myself, so I know that it's true! The earliest account of strange things falling from the sky appears in the Bible in the Book of Joshua. The Israelites, led by Joshua, have routed the Amorite army and are in pursuit of the survivors. A shower of stones falls from the sky and kills more of the enemy than those who died in battle. There are other biblical accounts of things falling from the sky, like the locusts and frogs that tormented Egypt.

About forty times a year, there are reports of creatures falling from the sky. Fish and frogs are the main culprits, having dropped out of the sky many times and in many places around the world.

In 2006, a fish encased in ice

It's raining spiders!

crashed through the windshield of a parked car at a marina in Seattle, Washington. Snakes, periwinkles, tadpoles, jellyfish, and even crabs have rained down many times—and often, still alive!

When a tornado passes over a lake or pond, it can sweep up objects of all shapes and sizes, and then drop them some distance away. Waterspouts have swept up different species of fish, eels, worms, birds, jellyfish, squid, and even alligators, carrying them many miles inland and depositing them on unsuspecting residents below, often encased in ice or hail.

Waterspouts and tornadoes can lift living creatures high into the clouds, where the temperature can be as cold as −60°F (16°C), and the animals become covered with ice. Sometimes the creatures fall to the ground alive but frightened. Often times the "deposit" happens in an area where the sun is out and the sky is blue, leaving everyone who witnessed the event to wonder what happened!

Here are some other reported occurrences:

✳ In 1995, Nellie Straw was driving through Scotland in a storm when hundreds of frogs pelted her car.

✳ In 1881, in Worcester, England, a thunderstorm brought down tons of periwinkles and crabs.

✳ In 1890, birds' blood rained down on Messignadi in Calabria, Italy.

✳ In 1877, several 1-foot-long alligators fell on J. L. Smith's farm in South Carolina.

✳ In November 1996, a town in southern Tasmania was slimed. Apparently it had rained either fish eggs or baby jellyfish.

✳ A Korean fisherman, trolling off the coast of the Falkland Islands, was knocked unconscious by a single frozen squid that fell from the sky.

✳ In 2004, Kate Walker of Dartford, England, got the shock of her life when twenty crabs rained down on her while she was gardening.

✳ In 1966, Father Leonard Bourne was dashing from a downpour across a courtyard in North Sydney, Australia, when a large fish fell from the sky and landed on his shoulder. The priest nearly caught it as it slid down his chest, but it squirmed away, fell to the flooded ground and swam away!

✳ In 1989, in Ipswich, Australia, Harold Degen's front lawn was covered with about eight hundred sardines that rained down from above in a light shower.

* In Chilatchee, Alabama, in 1956, a woman and her husband watched a small dark cloud form in an otherwise clear sky. When it was overhead, the cloud released its contents: rain, catfish, bass, and bream—all of the fish alive! What a dinner they must have had!

Great Tornado Web Sites >>>>

All about Tornadoes: www.tornadoproject.com/

www.crh.noaa.gov/lmk/ preparedness/tornado_large/ fslide1.php

www.whyfiles.org/013tornado/ index.html

www.nssl.noaa.gov/primer/ tornado/tor_basics.html

www.weatherwizkids.com/ tornado.htm

Frequently asked Tornado Questions: www.spc.noaa.gov/faq/ tornado/

Fujita EF Scale: www.spc.noaa.gov/ efscale/

All about Derechos and Straight-line Winds: www.spc.noaa.gov/ misc/AbtDerechos/derechofacts. htm

Tornado Graphics: www.usatoday. com/weather/tg/wtorwhat/ wtorwhat.htm

Try This at Home!

Make Your Own Tornado!

Tornado in a Box (Best!): www. tornadoproject.com/cellar/ workshop.htm

Tornado in a Bottle (Easier!): www.weatherwizkids.com/ tornado1.htm

Tornado in a Jar (Easiest!):www. weatherwizkids.com/tornado2. htm

Tornado in Another Box: wow. osu.edu/experiments/weather/ tornado.html

SECTION

2

HURRICANES

Hurricanes: Monsters of the Tropics

Hurricanes are the extreme-est of the extreme! Their winds and waves have wiped out entire communities worldwide and have changed coastal landscapes all over the planet. Hurricanes are the deadliest of storms with more than 20,000 American lives lost in the last 150 years. In a single year, as many as eighty-five hurricanes can prowl across the earth.

A hurricane is a gigantic machine, a tremendous latent heat pump, which can produce violent winds, incredible waves, torrential rains, tornadoes, and tremendous amounts of flooding.

What we call a hurricane is really a tropical cyclone, which is the generic term for a low-pressure system that generally forms in the tropics. The winds of a hurricane swirl around a calm central zone called an *eye*, which is surrounded by a band of tall, dark clouds called the *eyewall*. Pressure changes around the eyewall create the hurricane's strongest winds.

A washed-out bridge in the middle of a flood

When these storms happen over the northern Atlantic Ocean, the Caribbean Sea, the Gulf of Mexico, or the northeastern Pacific Ocean, they are called hurricanes. The word "hurricane" comes from "Hurican," the Carib god of evil. Hurican was derived from the Mayan god, Hurakan, one of the culture's creator gods, "who blew his breath across the chaotic water and brought forth dry land."

In other parts of the world, hurricanes have different names depending on where they occur. In the northwestern Pacific Ocean they are called typhoons. When their wind speeds exceed 150 mph they are called super typhoons. In the southwestern Pacific and southeastern Indian oceans they are called severe tropical cyclones; in the northern Indian Ocean they are called severe cyclonic storms; and in the southwestern Indian Ocean they are called tropical cyclones. Whew! That's a lot of descriptions from around the world. Sometimes you need a scorecard to keep up in this game!

Hurricanes are also the only natural disasters with their own names. Camille, Wilma, Charlie, Andrew, Hugo, Katrina—each seemed to have a personality and each caused a different sort of disaster.

Hurricanes are very special. A tornado can have winds up to 300 mph, but a hurricane is rarely above 155 mph. A tornado, however, is a very concentrated event compared to a hurricane. A tornado may be more violent, but hurricanes are more deadly! As you will see in this section, hurricanes *make* tornadoes!

A mile-wide tornado is huge, but a 100-mile-wide hurricane is considered small. Few tornadoes last an hour, whereas a hurricane can last for weeks, producing 12 to 20 inches of rain and flooding hundreds of miles of coastline with 20- to 30-foot-high storm surges.

Despite improved weather

forecasting of hurricanes, loss of life and terrible destruction continue to occur. This was never more evident than in Louisiana and Mississippi in August of 2005, when Hurricane Katrina caused the deaths of 1,836 people and the destruction of hundreds of thousands of homes and other buildings.

Hurricanes generate an incredible amount of energy. In one day, an average hurricane can produce the equivalent of 200 times the total amount of electricity that can be produced worldwide! That's an incredible amount of energy! Imagine if we could capture or harness that energy—we would never have to rely on fossil fuels again.

Fortunately, only about 3 percent of that energy is converted into wind and waves. I say *fortunately* because if all of that energy were converted to the surface landmass, it would have the destructive impact of all of the nuclear weapons of the United States and Russia put together!

Ingredients for a Hurricane

The ingredients for a hurricane are simple, yet the formation of a hurricane is a complex process. The key ingredient for a tropical cyclone is a little wind and some warm ocean

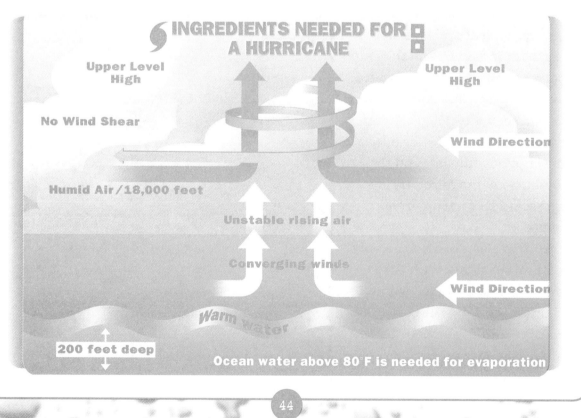

INGREDIENTS NEEDED FOR A HURRICANE

Upper Level High

Upper Level High

No Wind Shear

Wind Direction

Humid Air / 18,000 feet

Unstable rising air

Converging winds

Wind Direction

Warm Water

200 feet deep

Ocean water above 80°F is needed for evaporation

water—82°F (28°C) and above. Add a humid air mass and weak upper winds flowing in the same direction as those on the surface of the ocean, and you have the perfect environment for a tropical cyclone, especially if the surface winds are rotating.

Preexisting weather disturbances—like thunderstorms moving across from western Africa—can interact with rotating surface winds, a rising humid air mass, and higher-level winds fto create a tropical cyclone.

This sort of encounter takes place fairly often, but thankfully, only a few of these disturbances become full-blown hurricanes! I can watch the satellite loops all season long and see hundreds of these situations develop, but usually just a handful will have winds of above tropical storm strength at 39 mph!

The warm water must be at least 200 feet deep because as the storm develops, it forces energy into the ocean, which brings cold water up from the depths below.

Winds must be converging at the surface and the wind must also be unstable so that the growing storm will rise. The air must be very humid and go very high into the storm system (as high as 18,000 feet) as the extra water vapor supplies more energy.

To avoid ripping apart the developing storm, all existing winds should be coming from the same direction and at nearly the same speeds. Finally, an upper-atmospheric high-pressure area must exist above the system to pull away the air rising through the storm. This will help the storm to grow stronger.

I think you can understand now why only 10 percent of tropical disturbances grow into tropical storms. The combination of the right ingredients, coming together in the right conditions at the right time, is extremely rare!

Structure of a Tropical Cyclone

The formation of a tropical cyclone is also a process. First, thunderstorms grow and combine, creating a disturbed area in the tropics. Then warm humid air spirals inward as the thunderstorms organize into a circle or a swirl. Next, bands of thunderstorms spiral around the center. Hurricanes are made up of these bands of thunderstorms, called rain bands or spiral bands. They can be 3 to 30 miles wide, and 50 to 300 miles long. The spiral bands contain all of the destructive

HURRICANES OF THE TROPICS

The inside of a hurricane

Air flowing out from the center

Rising air

Storm Surge causes flooding before the hurricane's eye hits land

winds and flooding rains of a hurricane.

The most recognizable feature of any hurricane is the eye. This is an area, 10 to 40 miles in diameter, around which the entire storm rotates. In the eye, the skies are clear and the winds are light. It's the calmest part of the tropical cyclone, the area where the lowest surface pressures are found.

A hurricane's eye becomes visible when some of the rising air in the eyewall is forced toward the center of the storm from all directions. This convergence causes the air to actually sink in the eye. This creates a warmer environment and the clouds evaporate, leaving a clear area in the center.

Air flowing out from the center of the storm begins curving clockwise as water vapor in the air forms cirrostratus clouds, which cap the storm. As the storm approaches the coast of a landmass, a huge mound of water builds to the right of the eye. This is called the *storm surge*, which is discussed further later on.

These monster storms capture our attention because of their power and their destructive capabilities, as well as their impact on the economy and on our society.

How Water Powers a Hurricane

As I mentioned, a warm ocean and warm air are the key ingredients in a hurricane. The warmer the air, the better. Some of the largest and most destructive hurricanes of all time, like the 1938 hurricane called the "Long Island Express," and Hurricane Camille in 1969, occurred during years in which there was record heat.

Warm seawater evaporates and is absorbed by the surrounding air. As humid air rises high into the atmosphere, water vapor condenses into water drops. When that happens, heat is released. This is called *latent heat*—remember, earlier I described a hurricane as a latent heat pump. That latent heat warms the surrounding air, making it lighter and causing the air mass to rise even more. As the warm air rises, more air flows inward to replace it, causing wind.

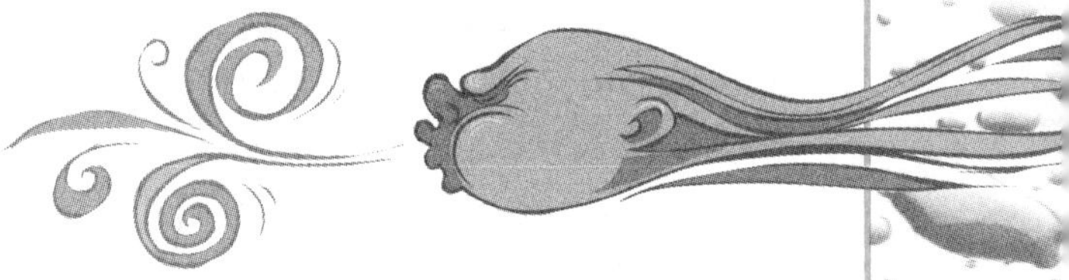

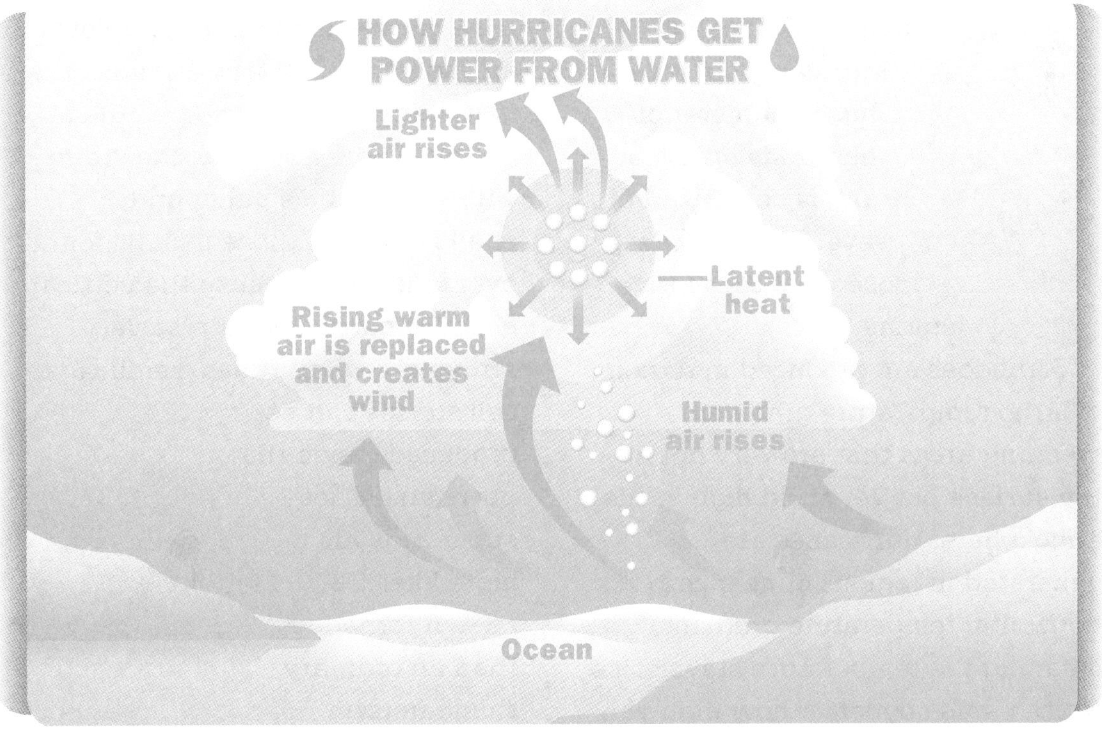

HOW HURRICANES GET POWER FROM WATER

Lighter air rises

Latent heat

Rising warm air is replaced and creates wind

Humid air rises

Ocean

Did You Know Hurricanes Produce Tornadoes? It's True!

While both hurricanes and tornadoes are atmospheric "vortices" (counterclockwise rotation of air), they have little in common. Most tornadoes have diameters of hundreds of feet and are produced from a single convective storm (i.e., a thunderstorm or cumulonimbus). A hurricane, however, has a diameter of hundreds of miles and is comprised of several, sometimes dozens, of convective storms.

Tornadoes are produced in regions of large temperature gradient, meaning areas that are very hot at the surface but very cold high in the atmosphere. Hurricanes are generated in regions of near zero horizontal temperature gradient, meaning the temperature stays close to the same no matter how high you go into the atmosphere. Tornadoes primarily develop over land because the sun's heating of the land surface usually contributes to the development of the thunderstorm that spawns the vortex. In contrast, hurricanes are purely oceanic phenomena—they die out over land due to a loss of their moisture source. Last, hurricanes have a lifetime that is measured in days, while tornadoes typically last for a number of heart-pounding minutes.

However, hurricanes can spawn tornadoes when certain instability and vertical shear (change of winds with height) conditions are met. In hurricanes, most of the thermal instability is found near or below an altitude of 10,000 feet. Because the instability in hurricanes occurs at relatively low altitudes, the storm cells tend to be smaller and shallower than those usually found over land. But because the vertical shear in hurricanes is also very strong at low altitudes, small super cell storms can be produced inside the hurricane. These super cells are more likely to spawn tornadoes than an ordinary thunderstorm.

Which Hurricane Is the Biggest Tornado Producer?

Hurricane Ivan in 2004 caused a multiday outbreak of 127 tornadoes. Most of the tornadoes occurred on September 17 in the mid-Atlantic region of the United States, two days after Ivan's landfall in Alabama. State-by-state tornado counts from Ivan include 40 in Virginia, 25 in Georgia, 22 in Florida, 9 in both Maryland and Pennsylvania, 8 in Alabama, 7 in South Carolina, 4 in North Carolina, and 3 in West Virginia. At least seven people were killed and seventeen injured by these tornadoes.

Who's the Most Damaging Tornado Producer?

One of the tornadoes produced by Hurricane Allen in 1980 did about $50 million worth of damage (in 1980 dollars; about $127 million in 2005 dollars) in the Austin, Texas, area.

More recently, Hurricane Cindy in July 2005 spawned a strong tornado that damaged the Atlanta Motor Speedway and other nearby areas to the tune of some $71.5 million (in 2005 dollars).

Storm Surge— The Biggest Killer

The most dangerous part of the hurricane is the rapid rise in the water's sea level; this is called the *storm surge.* The storm surge is caused by the swirling ocean winds driving the water onto the shore. A hurricane's winds force energy into the ocean, causing the water to pile up. The storm's winds push the

A storm surge during a hurricane

water inward, toward the right of the eye. When the hurricane is out at sea, that water spreads out harmlessly, but as the hurricane approaches land, this water becomes trapped between the shore and the hurricane itself. The sea level rises quickly: in just 2 to 3 hours, 20 feet or more of water can push inland. If the storm surge arrives at high tide, the water could rise even higher: up to 5 to 10 feet higher given the area where this occurs.

Let's say the normal high tide on the shoreline is 5 feet above mean sea level. Add 20 feet of water from a hurricane and you have a surge of 25 feet. If the storm surge were to come during an astronomical high tide (a greater-than-normal high tide caused by the gravitational effects of the moon), the effects would be even greater. The Galveston Hurricane of 1900 came ashore with a devastating storm surge; between 6,000 and 12,000 lives were lost, making it the deadliest disaster in the history of the United States.

Some of the factors that determine the height of the surge are the speed, intensity, and size of the wind field of the hurricane; the angle at which the hurricane approaches the coast; and the physical characteristics of the coastline. The worst effects of storm

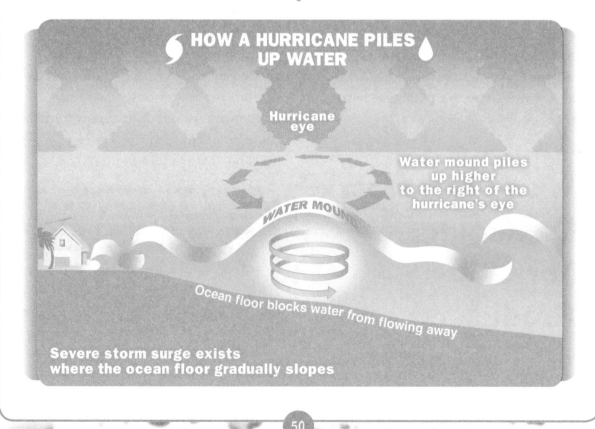

HOW A HURRICANE PILES UP WATER

Hurricane eye

Water mound piles up higher to the right of the hurricane's eye

WATER MOUND

Ocean floor blocks water from flowing away

Severe storm surge exists where the ocean floor gradually slopes surge occur where the ocean floor slopes gradually to the shore.

Because water is so much heavier than air, the storm surge causes even more damage than the hurricane's fierce winds. Since coastlines today are so densely populated, with too many homes built too close to the ocean, even the smallest storm surges can cause very serious property loss and loss of life.

Stages of Hurricane Development

Tropical Disturbance

Often called the birth of a hurricane, tropical disturbances are areas of showers and thunderstorms with a little wind circulation around an area of low pressure. They may have some towering cumulonimbus clouds and might last for more than 24 hours. In this picture, you can see a tropical disturbance that looks like a blob of puffy clouds. Beneath those clouds are a number of thunderstorms. A circular wind pattern is starting to take place. When meteorologists see a satellite picture like this—either a still or an animated loop—they know that it's likely that the disturbance will grow stronger.

Tropical Depression

A tropical depression is the next stage of a growing tropical system. In this picture, the low-pressure area, or "depression," is now surrounded by winds that have begun to blow in a circular pattern. At this point, the maximum wind speed will be 38 mph. The system will continue to draw in more warm, moist air, which will build more thunderstorms and feed existing ones. Meteorologists will plot the depression's path and watch it for signs that it is continuing to grow larger and stronger.

Tropical Storm

When a tropical depression's winds exceed 38 mph, it has become a tropical storm. The clouds have taken on a more well-defined, circular shape. Thunderstorm bands are flowing out from the center. Beneath this storm, the winds are so strong and the seas so rough, that ships must now avoid the area. A tropical storm's winds will range from 39 to 74 mph.

The storm is now drawing more heat and water vapor from the sea. It has a column of warm air near its center. As this column becomes warmer, air pressure at the ocean's surface falls. The falling pressure draws more air into the storm and the storm grows stronger.

This is the point in the storm's life where it is given a name.

Hurricane Dean

Hurricane

In these pictures of Hurricanes Felix and Dean, you can see a well-defined, concentric pattern of clouds and a well-formed eye. A storm achieves hurricane status when its winds are in excess of 74 mph. In the eyewall, warm air spirals upward, creating the hurricane's strongest winds. The speed of the winds in the eyewall is related to the diameter of the eye. A hurricane's winds blow faster if the eyewall is small; if the eye widens, the winds decrease.

The hurricane is now drawing large amounts of heat and moisture from the sea. Heavy rains are falling from the spiral or feeder bands—as much as 2 inches per hour—and the seas are churning dangerously as the storm surge builds!

Hurricane Felix approaches the East Coast
16 August 1995 2000 UTC
GOES-9 test image
2 km resolution
GOES Project NASA-GSFC

Hurricane Felix

How Do Hurricanes Get Their Names?

There's a great novel by George R. Stewart, *Storm*, which I assign to all my student interns. *Storm* is very popular among meteorologists. Written in 1941, and still relevant, it's about a forecaster who used women's names for naming storms.

The idea must have made quite an impact on weathermen; during World War II, military forecasters began to formally attach women's names to storms. Naming helps forecasters avoid confusion and keep track of the storms; it also helps researchers keep things straight. Most times during a hurricane season, there can be two or three storms at a time on the Atlantic and as many as two or three in the Pacific. That's a lot of storms, and giving them names makes it easier to track and keep up with them as well as to go back and research them later.

Each year, the World Meteorological Organization (WMO), an agency of the United Nations, issues four alphabetical lists of names for tropical storms. There's one list for the northern Atlantic Ocean and the Caribbean Sea, and one list for each of the regions of the Pacific Ocean: eastern, central, and northwestern. The lists include both men's and women's names that are popular in countries that might be affected by the storms in each area. As the equality movement prevailed across the United States, the practice of using men's and women's names was started in 1978 in the eastern Pacific and the following year in the Atlantic and Gulf of Mexico.

Except in the northwestern and central Pacific, the first storm of the year gets a name beginning with A— such as Tropical Storm Ana. If the storm intensifies into a hurricane, it becomes Hurricane Ana. The second storm gets a name beginning with B, and so on through the alphabet. The lists do not use all the letters of the alphabet since there are few names beginning with such letters as Q or U. Also, no Atlantic or Caribbean storms receive names beginning with Q, U, X, Y, or Z.

In the northwestern and central Pacific, the lists include names of animals and things as well as people. For instance, a typhoon was named after a cricket or a cicada in a certain country's language.

Atlantic/Caribbean Names

2009	2010	2011
Ana	Alex	Arlene
Bill	Bonnie	Bret
Claudette	Colin	Cindy
Danny	Danielle	Don
Erika	Earl	Emily
Fred	Fiona	Franklin
Grace	Gaston	Gert
Henri	Hermine	Harvey
Ida	Igor	Irene
Joaquin	Julia	Jose
Kate	Karl	Katia
Larry	Lisa	Lee
Mindy	Matthew	Maria
Nicholas	Nicole	Nate
Odette	Otto	Ophelia
Peter	Paula	Philippe
Rose	Richard	Rina
Sam	Shary	Sean
Teresa	Tomas	Tammy
Victor	Virginie	Vince
Wanda	Walter	Whitney

You Have Been Retired from the Game!

Hurricanes that have a severe impact on people's lives and are devastating to property and the economy become part of weather history, and are remembered for generations. When a storm of this magnitude occurs, any country affected by the storm can request that the storm's name be retired by the World Meteorological Organization. Here is a list of major Atlantic and Caribbean hurricanes whose names will no longer be used.

Hurricane Dennis

Retired Names

NAME	YEAR
Agnes	1972
Alicia	1983
Allen	1980
Allison	2001
Andrew	1992
Anita	1977
Audrey	1957
Betsy	1965
Beulah	1967
Bob	1991
Camille	1969
Carla	1961
Carmen	1974
Carol	1954
Celia	1970
Cesar	1996
Charley	2004
Cleo	1964
Connie	1955
David	1979
Dean	2007
Dennis	2005
Diana	1990

NAME	YEAR		NAME	YEAR
Diane	1955		Ione	1955
Donna	1960		Iris	2001
Dora	1964		Isabel	2003
Edna	1968		Isidore	2002
Elena	1985		Ivan	2004
Eloise	1975		Janet	1955
Fabian	2003		Jeanne	2004
Felix	2007		Joan	1988
Fifi	1974		Juan	2003
Flora	1963		Katrina	2005
Floyd	1999		Keith	2000
Fran	1996		Klaus	1990
Frances	2004		Lenny	1999
Frederic	1979		Lili	2002
Georges	1998		Luis	1995
Gilbert	1988		Marilyn	1995
Gloria	1985		Michelle	2001
Gustav	2008		Mitch	1998
Hattie	1961		Noel	2007
Hazel	1954		Opal	1995
Hilda	1964		Paloma	2008
Hortense	1996		Rita	2005
Hugo	1989		Roxanne	1995
Ike	2008		Stan	2005
Inez	1966		Wilma	2005

Hurricane Katrina

The Saffir-Simpson Hurricane Scale

I'm sure you've heard of hurricanes being rated on some sort of scale. You hear people say, "That storm is a 1," or "That one is a Category 2," and so on. Those numbers are from the Saffir-Simpson Scale. This scale was formulated in 1969, after Hurricane Camille slaughtered the Mississippi Gulf Coast. The damage from that hurricane was quite shocking, at least in part because there was, at that

SAFFIR-SIMPSON SCALE ▫ OF HURRICANE DAMAGE ▫

Category 1
Minimal Damage
Wind Speeds: 74–95 mph
Storm Surge: 4–5 feet

Category 2
Moderate Damage
Wind Speeds: 96–110 mph
Storm Surge: 6–8 feet

Category 3
Extensive Damage
Wind Speeds: 111–130 mph
Storm Surge: 9–12 feet

Category 4
Extreme Damage
Wind Speeds: 131–155 mph
Storm Surge: 13–18 feet

Category 5
Catastrophic Damage
Wind Speeds: More Than 155 mph
Storm Surge: More Than 18 feet

time, no way to predict a storm's potential impact. The population had no sense of what to expect from a hurricane of Camille's mammoth strength and size.

Dr. Robert Simpson, who at the time was director of the National Hurricane Center in Miami, realized the need to help disaster agencies better understand how much damage a particular storm might cause. So he called on Herbert Saffir, a consulting engineer who, Simpson says, was "well known as the father of the Miami building code." Simpson handled the meteorology part, and Saffir the engineering part, of developing a new hurricane damage assessment tool.

The two came up with the Saffir-Simpson Damage-Potential Scale, which assigns each hurricane a rating, from 1 to 5, based on the storm's intensity. This scale is used to estimate the potential property damage and flooding expected along the coast from a hurricane landfall. Wind speed is the only determining factor in the scale; after all, projecting storm surge heights are difficult due to the varied slope of the continental shelf and the shape of the coastline in the area where the hurricane makes landfall.

CATEGORY 1 HURRICANE

Winds 74 to 95 mph (64 to 83 kt). This is a minimal hurricane that brings a small storm surge, generally 4 to 5 feet above normal. However, this relatively small surge should not be taken lightly, as the time of the storm's arrival and the shape of the coastline are major factors. For example, if the storm arrives at high tide, then the surge will be higher.

There's little chance of serious damage to buildings in a storm this size. However, there will be some damage to various sorts of structures, especially unanchored mobile homes, and shrubbery and trees, which take a beating. Signs will be blown down as well as some power lines. At the beach or along the coast there will be some flooding of roads and minor damage to piers.

CATEGORY 2 HURRICANE

Winds 96 to 110 mph (83 to 96 kt). This is where you begin to see significant damage to the roofs, doors, and windows of buildings.

There's also considerable damage to mobile homes, piers, and to poorly constructed signs on buildings and along roads. The storm surge can be as high as 5 to 10 feet at the normal high tide. Coastal roads and escape routes flood 2 to 4 hours before the arrival of the hurricane's center. Small boats in unprotected anchorages break their moorings and go flying.

CATEGORY 3 HURRICANE

Winds 111 to 130 mph (96 to 113 kt). Once a storm becomes a Category 3, it is considered major. The storm surge is generally 9 to 12 feet above normal with structural damage to residences and other buildings. Mobile homes and most signs are destroyed. Many plants are stripped of their foliage and even large trees are blown down.

Low-lying roads and evacuation routes are cut by rising water 3 to 5 hours before arrival of the center of the hurricane. Flooding near the coast destroys smaller homes and buildings; larger structures are damaged, battered by floating debris. Areas where the land is lower than 5 feet above mean sea level may be flooded for 8 miles or more inland. Residents in these areas will have to be evacuated, especially those within several blocks of the shoreline.

CATEGORY 4 HURRICANE

Winds 131 to 155 mph (114 to 135 kt). At this point, the storm surge is generally 13 to 18 feet above normal! There's more extensive destruction with some complete roof structure failures on small residences. There's complete destruction of mobile homes and extensive damage to doors and windows of permanent structures. Major damage occurs to lower floors of structures near the shore. Shrubs, trees, and all signs are blown down.

Low-lying escape routes may be cut by rising water 3 to 5 hours before

A flooded forest after a storm

the arrival of the center of the hurricane. Any area of land lower than 10 feet above sea level may be flooded, requiring massive evacuation of residential areas as far inland as 6 miles!

CATEGORY 5 HURRICANE

Winds greater than 155 mph (135 kt). Whoa! This is the top of the scale! The storm surge is generally greater than 18 feet above normal. Roofs on nearly all residences and industrial buildings will be completely destroyed. Larger structures will be shattered while smaller ones will be blown away. Your mobile home is gone!

There will be severe and extensive window and door damage to inland homes and buildings. There's also major damage to the lower floors of all buildings located less than 15 feet above sea level and within 500 yards of the shoreline. All shrubs, trees, and signs will be blown down.

Low-lying escape routes are cut by rising water 3 to 5 hours before the arrival of the center of the hurricane. There will be massive evacuation of residential areas on low ground within 5 to 10 miles of the shoreline.

Only three Category 5 hurricanes have made landfall in the United States since records began: the Labor Day Hurricane of 1935 (remember, the naming of hurricanes did not begin until the 1940s), Hurricane Camille in 1969, and Hurricane Andrew in August 1992. The 1935 Labor Day Hurricane struck the Florida Keys with a minimum barometric pressure of 892 millibars (mb)—the lowest pressure of a hurricane at landfall ever observed in the United States. The lower the pressure, the stronger and nastier the storm will be.

When Hurricane Camille struck the Mississippi Gulf Coast, it caused a 25-foot storm surge, which inundated Pass Christian. Hurricane Katrina, a Category 5 storm over the Gulf of Mexico, was responsible for at least 81 billion dollars of property damage when it struck the Gulf Coast as a Category 3. Katrina is by far the costliest hurricane to ever strike the United States.

Hurricane Wilma of 2005 was a Category 5 hurricane at its peak intensity. Wilma is the strongest Atlantic tropical cyclone on record, with a minimum pressure of 882 mb. Fortunately, it did not make landfall at peak intensity! Wilma was a Category 3 as the time of her landfall.

Hurricane Katrina

Deadliest Tropical Storms in U.S. History, Resulting in Fifty or More Deaths

DEATHS	LOCATION	DATE
8,000+	Galveston, TX	September 1900
2,500+	Lake Okeechobee, FL	September 1928
1,000–2,500	SC, GA	August 1893
1,800–2,000	Coastal LA and MS	October 1896
1,836	(Hurricane Katrina) LA, MS	August 2005
700+	GA, SC	August 1881
638	New England	September 1938
600+	Florida (marine)	September 1919
500+	GA, SC	September 1804
450+	Corpus Christi, TX	September 1919
424	NC Capes (marine)	September 1857
408	Florida Keys	September 1935
400	Île Dernière, LA	August 1856
390	New England	September 1944
390	(Hurricane Audrey) west LA	June 1957
350+	Grand Isle, LA	September 1909
300	South Carolina	September 1922
275	New Orleans, LA	September 1915
275	Upper coast of Texas	August 1925
256	(Hurricane Camille) MS, VA	August 1969

DEATHS	LOCATION	DATE
243	Florida	September 1926
184	(Hurricane Diane) NC to ME	September 1955
179	Georgia coast	October 1898
176	Indianola, TX	September 1875
164	Southeast Florida	October 1906
134	FL, AL, and MS	September 1906
122	(Tropical Storm Agnes) PA, NY	June 1972
100+	Sabine, TX	October 1886
100	Florida	September 1896
95	(Hurricane Hazel) NY, NJ	October 1954
90+	SC, NC (marine)	October 1837
75	Hurricane Betsy (FL, LA)	September 1965
70	Brownsville, TX	August 1844
68	Florida	October 1896
60	(Hurricane Carol) MA, ME	August 1954
57	(Hurricane Hugo) SC, NC	September 1989
53	(Hurricane Floyd) NC to NJ	September 1999
52	(Hurricane Ivan) AL, FL	September 2004
51	San Antonio, TX	September 1921
51	Southeast Florida, LA, MS	September 1947
50	South Florida	November 1925

Costliest Hurricanes

RANK	NAME	YEAR	CATEGORY	DAMAGE (IN BILLIONS)
1	Katrina (LA/MS/AL/SE FL)	2005	3	$100
2	Andrew (SE FL/SE LA)	1992	5	$35
3	Wilma (FL)	2005	3	$21
4	Charley (FL)	2004	4	$14
5	Ivan (FL/AL)	2004	3	$13
6	Rita (LA/TX)	2005	3	$10
7	Hugo (SC)	1989	4	$9.8
8	Frances (FL)	2004	2	$8.9
9	Agnes (NE US)	1972	1	$8.6
10	Betsy (FL/LA)	1965	3	$8.5
11	Camille (MS/AL)	1969	5	$7.0
12	Jeanne (FL)	2004	3	$6.5
13	Georges (PR/MS)	1998	5	$6.3
14	Diane (NE US)	1955	1	$5.5
15	Allison (TX/LA)	2001	Tropical Storm	$5.0
16	Frederic (AL/MS)	1979	3	$5.0
17	Great New England	1938	3	$4.8
18	Floyd (NC)	1999	4	$4.7
19	Fran (NC)	1996	3	$3.7
20	Opal (NW FL/AL)	1995	3	$3.6

EAST COAST HURRICANES—HIGHEST WIND SPEEDS IN ATLANTIC TROPICAL STORMS

SPEED	DATE	LOCATION	STORM NAME
186 mph	September 21, 1938	Blue Hill Observatory, MA	Great New England
178 mph	September 6, 1965	Great Abaco Is., Bahamas	Betsy
175 mph	September 27, 1955	Chetumal, Mexico	Janet
175 mph	September 11, 1961	Port Lavaca, TX	Carla
174 mph	August 24, 1992	Coral Gables, FL	Andrew
172 mph	August 17, 1969	Boothville, LA	Camille
163 mph	October 18, 1944	Havana, Cuba	unnamed
160 mph	September 13, 1928	San Juan, Puerto Rico	unnamed
155 mph	September 17, 1947	Hillsboro Lighthouse, FL	unnamed

The Most Extreme Wind Anywhere in the World!

A wind gust of 190 mph was measured by the weather station on the island of Miyako-jima in the Ryukyu Islands chain on September 5, 1966. This is the highest wind speed ever measured in a tropical storm anywhere in the world!

Pacific Hurricanes

Atlantic Ocean hurricanes affect the Caribbean, the Gulf of Mexico, and the eastern coast of the United States, whereas Pacific hurricanes affect the western coast of the United States and Mexico, the Far East (the eastern edge of China, plus Japan, Taiwan, and all other nations with coastlines along the Pacific Ocean), and islands in the Pacific, like Hawaii. In the Far East, hurricanes are called typhoons; Australians like to call them "willy-willies."

The Pacific hurricane/typhoon seasons are May 15 to November 30 for the eastern Pacific (western Mexico, Baja California, California, Oregon, Washington, British Columbia, Alaska, Russia); June 1 to November 30 for the central Pacific (western Mexico, western Latin America, Hawaii, Polynesia, Micronesia, and central Pacific islands); October 15 to May 15 for the southwest Pacific/Australian basin; and year-round for the northwest Pacific basin.

Eastern Pacific storms originate just north of the equator, off the western coasts of Mexico and Central America, in places where the water reaches temperatures of 80°F or more. These hurricanes then move north to northwest, into the central Pacific. While a hurricane proper has never hit the coast of California, remnants of hurricanes have. Most hurricanes weaken as they near the California coast because the water temperature there is 60°F (156°C) year-round, which weakens the storms considerably.

The Tops in Central Pacific Hurricanes

STRENGTH	NAME	DATE
Category 5 (173 miles/150 kt)	John	August 1994
Category 5 (173 miles/150 kt)	Patsy	September 1959
Category 5 (161 miles/140 kt)	Ioke	August 2006
Category 5 (161 miles/140 kt)	Emilia	July 1994
Category 5 (161 miles/140 kt)	Gilma	July 1994
Category 4 (144 miles/125 kt)	Iniki	September 1992
Category 4 (144 miles/125 kt)	Rick	September 1985
Cateogry 4 (138 miles/120 kt)	Fabio	August 1988

THESE WERE "BIGGER THAN A PINEAPPLE" OVER HAWAII!

YEAR	HURRICANE NAME
1992	Iniki
1982	Iwa
1959	Dot
1957	Nina
1871	The Kohala Cyclone

The Hurricane Hunters

"Dude, are you *nuts*? You're going to take a perfectly good airplane and do *what*? Fly it through a hurricane? You're one taco short of a combo plate!"

There's a group of pilots called Hurricane Hunters, who have flown directly into some of the most violent hurricanes in recorded history. The

53rd Weather Reconnaissance Squadron is a U.S. Air Force Reserve group that is based in Biloxi, Mississippi.

The 53rd began flying in 1944, and they have shown that flying into hurricanes is safer than you might think. Altogether, only four planes have gone down: three Air Force craft in Pacific Ocean typhoons and one Navy plane in an Atlantic hurricane. Sadly, all thirty-six men aboard the four aircraft were lost. That's not to say that other planes haven't been badly shaken, and there have been a few injuries. On August 23, 1964, Hurricane Cleo shook a Navy Super Constellation so hard the Navy decided to scrap the airplane after looking at the damage!

The Hurricane Hunters fly directly

into hurricanes—that's right, not over or around, but *through*. They bore in from the outer edge all the way to the eye at the storm's center and out the other side. They gather information about the strength and makeup of the hurricane for forecasts and research—and to save lives. This vital information is sent back to the National Hurricane Center, where forecasters will use the data as the basis for forecasting where the hurricane is expected to travel and how strong it might become.

The dropsonde station

The Weather Reconaissance Squadron flies planes with a six-person crew: a commander, a co-pilot, a flight engineer, a navigator, a weather officer, and a dropsonde operator. A dropsonde is a weather-sensing canister attached to a parachute. This instrument, dropped from the plane as it flies through the storm, falls all the way through the hurricane to the ocean below. As the canister falls, it radios back information on temperature, humidity, and winds inside the storm. The WC-130 aircraft also has instruments to record wind speed inside the hurricane, as well as radar to see the thunderstorms.

Another group, the NOAA Hurricane Hunters, also does surveillance, research, and reconnaissance with their own specially equipped aircraft: a WP-3D Orion and a very cool Gulfstream IV SP jet. The jet can get to a storm quicker than the WP-3D Orion turboprop planes that are the Hurricane Hunters' primary aircraft, thereby sending information back faster. The Gulfstream IV is flown over the tops of hurricanes and around a storm's sides. It records the steering winds so a storm's path can be better predicted. Flying this jet into a hurricane would be dangerous, as the wind turbulence inside the hurricane would disrupt the jet's engines. That's why turboprop planes are used to penetrate a hurricane.

Even today's supermodern satellites cannot give us all the data necessary to forecast where a hurricane will go and when it will hit. Especially vulnerable would be oceangoing ships, which are too slow to outrun a hurricane. The only way to collect information about wind speed and the barometric pressure inside a hurricane is to fly a plane through it.

The rising or falling of the barometric pressure in a hurricane determines the strength or weakness of the storm. If the pressure is falling, the storm gets stronger and if the pressure is rising, it gets weaker. That data is necessary to accurately predict a hurricane's strength as well as its movement.

The Hurricane Hunters fly in the northern Atlantic and the northeastern Pacific. They have also been asked to fly into typhoons on occasion. The typhoons of the Pacific have been recorded as the strongest storms on earth. Dude, can you say "air sickness bag"?

My Flight with the Hurricane Hunters— or, How to Keep from Blowing Lunch!

I have to admit that I am an adrenaline junky. You qualify for the "adrenaline junkies club" if you are a person who loves to ride every ride at the amusement park, bungee jump, parachute, scuba dive with sharks, or fly in stunt planes. I've done all that stuff and even flown with the Blue Angels. Before each experience, I get very nervous, or, basically, scared. Fear is good, it keeps you focused!

My favorite thrill ride of them all is flying with the Hurricane Hunters. Why? Because this ride combines the science of meteorology (which I love) with nature's most awesome force—a hurricane. The ride is one part science lab and one part the Aerosmith ride at Disney World!

Imagine if you could ride a roller coaster during a hurricane: it would be strange, dangerous, and not very smart, but awesome if you're crazy and know the ride operator. There's something about flying into a Category 5 hurricane with winds of over 160 mph that strikes a certain fear in you, making your heart pound in your chest.

Our flight originated from Biloxi, Mississippi, the home of the Hurricane Hunters. Our flight commander was young, blond, rugged, calm, and had a fearless swagger to go along with his eyes of blue steel. He was everything you wanted in a leader. He had flown bombing missions for the Air Force in the Gulf War with Iraq. He looked every bit like a *Top Gun* pilot. I didn't ask, but he must have had one of those movie names like "Striker," "Lightning," or better yet, "Hurricane."

He reminded me of the actor Val Kilmer, whose character in the movie *Top Gun* was named "Iceman." Looking at him, I immediately thought of yelling out Tom Cruise's famous line from that movie, "I feel the need, the need for speed!" I was incredibly nervous, but remained calm in front of him because at that moment I realized I was about to make a complete fool of myself.

Commander Iceman gave you the feeling that you could trust him with your life. That was a good thing because I was scared to death. My prior experience with hurricanes came from reporting on them from a nice, climate-controlled studio, not having a personal encounter with the single greatest natural force on Earth.

As a reporter, I had struggled to stay on my feet during several storms that were at tropical storm strength, with winds of around 65 mph. But that would be nothing when compared to the experience of being inside a craft that was planning exploratory surgery inside a hurricane, especially when I

thought about the scale of what I was about to attempt. The very large WC-130 turboprop I would be flying in was about the size of a pinhead when compared to the gargantuan size of a hurricane.

I knew that no human can stand up in hurricane-force winds (74 mph). And though I knew the Hurricane Hunters flew their tiny, fragile planes through these killer storms all the time, I knew just how dangerous that was. I was petrified. We were about to fly through one of the strongest hurricanes in the history of the North Atlantic in a pea-size tin can.

I asked Commander Iceman, "What should I eat before a flight like this?" He said, "Bananas." I said, "Why bananas?" Iceman coolly replied, "Tastes the same coming back up."

Yes, We Have No Bananas

Hurricane Mitch formed off the African coast on October 10, 1998. Commander Iceman cruised westward through the Atlantic for a time in some unfavorable conditions until he reached the Caribbean Sea, south of Jamaica. Unfavorable wind shear high above the Atlantic had kept Mitch disorganized, but the conditions of the Caribbean were to his liking. Soon the upper-level shear was gone, Mitch's thunderstorms grew stronger, and he was on his way to stardom. Mitch was 295 miles south of Jamaica on the 24th when he grew rapidly from a Category 1 hurricane to a Category 5 hurricane.

By the 26th, Mitch's winds were up to 180 mph, and gusting to 200 mph, making Mitch the seventh-strongest hurricane of all time.

And we were about to fly right into it!

We strapped ourselves into bench seats in an area in the back of the WC-130 and got ready for takeoff. All of a sudden, the back end of the plane opened, and I could see the runway. The flight engineer, a young woman who was talking into a headset, was standing on the door that had dropped down, opening the entire back of the airplane. I asked her, "What's going on?"

"This is how we back the aircraft away for takeoff," she said. "I tell the commander how far he can back up the aircraft." I thought, gee, no rearview mirror for the Iceman?

Are We There Yet? Are We There Yet? Are We There Yet?

It was going to be about a ten-hour flight—four hours flying time each way to and from the storm and about an hour exploring Mitch's insides. The waiting was the hardest part. I was excited, anxious, nervous, and scared—all rolled into one. I was working hard to keep it together. In contrast, the flight crew was calm and very cool.

I looked out the window at the beautiful sunshine and the gorgeous waters of the

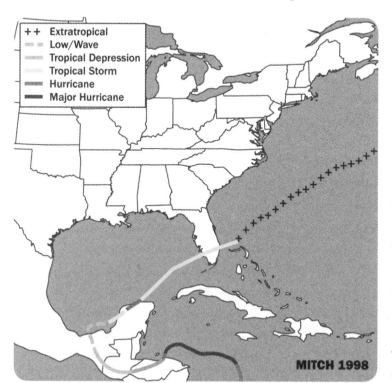

++ Extratropical
Low/Wave
Tropical Depression
Tropical Storm
Hurricane
Major Hurricane

MITCH 1998

Hurricane Mitch's track through the Gulf and the Caribbean

Gulf of Mexico and kept thinking that soon, all you-know-what would be breaking loose! I was still amazed at the thought that we were purposefully flying into one of the strongest hurricanes ever.

Who ever first came up with that idea? Well, it was the result of a bet!

A surprise hurricane that struck Houston, Texas, during World War II in 1943 marked the first intentional flight into a hurricane.

In the summer of that year, British pilots were being trained in instrument flying at Bryan Field in Houston. Using instruments to fly airplanes was new to the military; before, they would just look out the cockpit window. But what do you do if you're fogged in? You look at the instruments—the air speed indicator, the horizon, and the altimeter, to name a few—and fly the plane. Commercial pilots had been flying that way for a while, and now the military was learning to use their techniques.

As the hurricane approached, the British pilots saw that the Americans were evacuating their AT-6 Texan trainers in the face of the storm. They began teasing and taunting the Americans about the construction and air-worthiness of their planes. They basically said, "Dude, your planes stink and you're chicken!

Betcha won't fly one of your fine American planes in that storm!"

Lead instructor Colonel Joe Duckworth took the bet. He was smart and cool, like Commander Iceman. Duckworth wasn't a swashbuckling, devil-may-care World War II flyboy. He was a former airline pilot who knew how to use instruments to fly and was teaching the Army air forces how to fly through bad weather.

Duckworth and his navigator, Lt. Ralph O'Hair, took one of the trainers, flew directly into the eye of the storm, and returned safely. Word of what they had done spread around the base, and the base's weather officer, Lt. William Jones-Burdick, decided he wanted to fly into the storm. He took over the navigator's seat, and Duckworth flew through the storm a second time. This proved that hurricane reconnaissance flights were possible. The British pilots lost the bet and had to pay for everybody's dinner!

Holy Moly! There He Blows!

The beautiful sunlight was fading fast. In the distance, we could see Mitch. Mitch looked mad, *very* mad. He was a very tight, compact hurricane, with an eye 22 miles wide.

The calm blue sea that I had been looking at just minutes earlier now appeared to be boiling.

Commander Iceman told me that hurricanes that are spread out over many miles are not so bumpy. It's the tightly wound ones that give you the rough ride.

Okay José! We were headed toward the Yucatán Peninsula of Central America, where Mitch was going to crash-land with full Category 5 force.

"Everybody tighten your seat belts, we are going to pay Mitch a visit," was the word over the headsets from Commander Iceman. He sounded so calm and soothing, as if we were on one of those tourist flights around the Grand Canyon.

We were not going to fly through Mitch once, oh no, we were going to fly through six times! On our first pass, we would fly from the southwest part of the storm through the eye and out through the northeast, as if drawing a line through the storm from lower left to upper right.

What a doozy of a ride it was! The bumping and dipping starts out gently and becomes greater as you near the eyewall, which is the strongest part of the storm. We would be passing right through the strongest part of Mitch's 180+ mph

winds in the upper right, northeast quadrant of the hurricane. *Boo yah!*

Turbulence was causing our WC-130 to drop up and down with great force. You know how when you are on a commercial airplane and it bounces up and down a bit on takeoff or midflight? Imagine that times ten! My jaws were banging, teeth were rattling, stomach was swishing . . . oh, that breakfast. . . .

My fillings were being knocked out of my head. Nobody told me this ride would require a mouthpiece!

I noticed that the crew was calm and collected, just going about their business. Did I see a card game break out in the cockpit? They're way too cool up there.

The weather officer was taking readings from the instruments connected to the aircraft, measuring temperature, humidity, and flight-level wind speed. There are all kinds of cool instruments attached to the aircraft and there's radar in the nose cone.

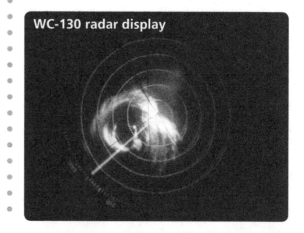

WC-130 radar display

Today's planes are equipped with highly sophisticated sensors to precisely detect hurricane winds. Sensors on the wings pick up radiation from sea foam caused by surface winds. The difference of a few miles per hour can be critical in determining a storm's damage potential.

The dropsonde operator was putting the small tubes called *radiosondes* into the large tube that ejects them from the bottom of the airplane. Radiosondes are lightweight digital radios that use GPS for positioning and wind-finding. The computer display immediately showed the information that was coming back from the radiosondes as they fell through Mitch before splashing into the water and cutting off.

On the computer, I could see that Mitch was a bad boy, with winds of 180 mph and gusts to 201! Dozens of radiosondes were deployed during our half-dozen or so passes, sending back crucial information that would hopefully save people's lives.

The ride was rough times ten—bouncing around, lightning flashing everywhere, lashing rain—until we hit the eyewall. Once we punched through, conditions were completely different. The air was calm and the weather was clear. I looked up and saw blue sky above us and the other

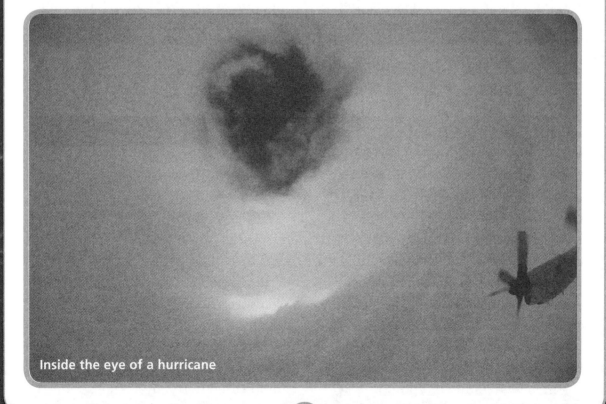

Inside the eye of a hurricane

side of the eyewall in front of me. What a ride!

Soon the calmness was over as we entered Mitch's strongest part, the northeast quadrant.

Holy cow! The engines just made some kind of wowing, whirling noise as we hit the large intestine of Mitch. It's as if the airplane is in the hand of a small child, zooming us around, up and down like a toy!

Looking out the window at the left wing tip, I saw a bright ball of blue-white light, like fireworks, a giant sparkler.

It's St. Elmo's fire!

St. Elmo's fire forms on aircraft wing tips, antennae, the tail, nose, and propeller blades. It has also been seen atop ship masts, tips of trees, tops of power poles, grass blades, and has even been seen glowing on the tips of the horns of cattle. It's rare and only happens when the atmosphere is superelectrically charged, as in a storm like Mitch. It's heatless and nonconsuming, and can last for minutes. It's beautiful, but scary.

Ancient Mediterranean sailors believed Elmo to be their patron saint. Many people believe that the appearance of St. Elmo's fire is a guiding hand during a terrible storm. They believed that the ghostly, dancing flame is a sign that the storm is weakening or ending.

Iceman's cool voice comes over the headset, telling me that it won't hurt our aircraft. He also said St. Elmo's fire can sometimes be heard singing on the aircraft's radio, a frying or hissing sound running up and down the musical scale.

Iceman then added, in his smooth, resonant baritone, that it's actually a sign that lightning is about to strike the plane.

What!?!

Blammo! You guessed it! Lightning just zapped the plane. We took a big dip.

Hey, we just took Mitch's best shot and we're doing fine . . . except for my stomach. Whoa! If only they had this ride at Disney World! They could call it the "Whirl and Puke."

I don't know if St. Elmo's fire is a good sign or not; it was certainly quite the show and a big hit with the crew.

Minutes later, we exit the upper right of Mitch to smoother air and our first pass is complete. Oh boy! Only five more times to go!

Five passes through Mitch later, my face is green and my hollowed eyes are rolled back in my head. How do these people do this for a living? Would someone please come and put me out of my misery?

Mitch tossed me around like a wet dishrag. I had the great pleasure of filling three hefty airsickness bags. I tossed not only my big breakfast, but lunch and dinner from the day before. I launched things I had eaten in previous decades. I threw up my great-grandmother's meat loaf that I ate in 1967. I was soaked in sweat right through my flight suit.

To top it off, Iceman resonates through my headset, "You did great; you only passed out for about ten minutes."

Thanks, Iceman.

The crew was amazing. This was like a day at the beach for them. I am so thankful they are on our weather team!

I read the written report that was sent back to the Hurricane Center. It had all the usual information about the conditions of Mitch during the flight: wind speed, strongest convection, eyewall characteristics, and so on. There was one little footnote at the end—something they almost never do: talk about how the ride went. The weather officer wrote that "though a rough ride, all managed to 'stomach' the trip." All but one that is! I was glad he didn't sell me out.

As for Mitch, he went on to be one of the deadliest and most powerful hurricanes on record in the Atlantic basin. At the time, Mitch was the fourth-most-intense hurricane in recorded history. It currently ranks seventh. Mitch dropped historic amounts of rainfall in Honduras and Nicaragua. Most official reports placed the rainfall at 3 feet. There were some unofficial reports of 75 inches!

Deaths due to the catastrophic flooding and mudslides made Mitch the second-deadliest Atlantic hurricane in history; 11,000 people were killed and more than 8,000 were classified as missing. That's a total somewhere in the neighborhood of 19,000 lives lost!

After Honduras and Nicaragua, Mitch made a right turn back toward the Gulf of Mexico, brushing the north coast of the Yucatán, and making a bead for South Florida. Though by this time Mitch was losing strength, he still had some wallop left.

With a 4-foot storm surge and sustained winds of 40 mph, Mitch dropped 7 to 10 inches of rain and five tornadoes on South Florida. Mitch destroyed 645 houses, injuring 65 people, and killing others who drowned when their boats capsized.

Because of Mitch's destruction in Central America and Florida, the World Meteorological Organization retired his name in the spring of 1999; it will never be used again for an Atlantic hurricane.

This is Iceman, requesting permission to fly by the tower . . .

Differences Between Hurricanes and Tornadoes

While both hurricanes and tornadoes are atmospheric vortices (a vortex is a counterclockwise rotation of air), they have little in common. Tornadoes are produced from a single convective storm, as explained in the tornado section of this book, and most are no more than hundreds of feet wide. Hurricanes are made up of many convective storms and are hundreds of miles wide.

Tornadoes are produced in regions of large temperature gradient, meaning that it's very hot at the surface of the land but changes gradually to very cold high in the atmosphere above. Hurricanes are generated in regions of near zero horizontal temperature gradient, meaning that the temperature is consistent throughout the air column.

While some tornadoes form over water, the majority of tornadoes form over land; the sun's heating of the earth's surface usually contributes to the development of the thunderstorm that spawns the vortex. In contrast, hurricanes are purely oceanic phenomena. They die out over land due to losing their source of moisture—the ocean.

Last, hurricanes take days to develop, do their destructive business, and disintegrate, while tornadoes typically last for only minutes.

The Greatest Storm on Earth

The most powerful storm ever recorded on the Earth's surface—since we've been able to keep track of these things—was Super Typhoon Tip, which formed in the western Pacific Ocean on October 5, 1979. Between classes—I was in college at the time, attending Mississippi State University—I watched the reports of this storm as closely as I could.

Slow to develop and exceedingly erratic in its early movement, Tip eventually grew into a monster storm with a cloud formation of 1,350 miles in diameter. If the storm had been centered in the Gulf of Mexico, it would have stretched from Miami, Florida, to Amarillo, Texas.

Dude, that is *huge*!

Tip's gale-force winds extended

out from its eye for a radius of 683 miles, about five times greater than a typical Atlantic hurricane. At its peak on October 12, the air pressure in the eye fell to 870 millibars (25.69 inches of mercury), the lowest ever measured at sea on the planet. This is the equivalent of what normal air pressure would be like at 2,500 feet.

Winds circulating around Tip's eye were blowing at a sustained rate of 190 mph, with gusts probably well over 200 mph. The eyewall extended up to 55,000 feet, where infrared temperatures were measured at an incredible −135°F (−92.8°C). Fortunately, Tip never made landfall, though it took a shot at Guam, swerving at the last moment to the west and thus sparing the small and vulnerable island.

By October 18, Tip had accelerated toward the northwest and was rapidly losing power. By the time it brushed Japan on October 19 and 20, it was much tamer. Wind gusts were only 88 mph along the runways at Tokyo's airport.

There have been other storms with lower air pressure. Cyclone Monica, which struck Australia's north coast in April 2006, now holds the world record for lowest pressure for any cyclone at 868.5 mb (25.65 inches of mercury). Meteorologists would expect this level of air pressure to be related to estimated winds of 180 mph, with gusts to 220 mph. However, when Monica struck the unpopulated area of northern Australia, there were no weather instruments in place to provide an official record of her wind speeds.

In the Atlantic Ocean, 1988's Hurricane Gilbert's 888 mb (26.22 inches of mercury) had retained the record for the lowest estimated pressure for more than a decade. I flew aboard the Hurricane Hunter during that hurricane and what a ride that was! However, Gilbert's record was eclipsed by Hurricane Wilma's 882 mb (26.04 inches of mercury) in October 2005.

However, despite these achievements in low air pressure, no other cyclone has ever reached the size and scope of Super Typhoon Tip.

Hurricane Extremes!

LARGEST EYE—EYE SEE YOU!

Wow! That's a big peeper you've got there!

Super Typhoon Carmen holds the record for the largest eye at 230 miles in diameter. That's a massive eye!

Despite that giant eye, the storm was relatively weak for its size. By the time it passed over Okinawa, Japan, on August 20, 1960, Carmen's winds were 90 mph.

Remember what I said earlier: when the eye is large, the storm will be weaker. Dynamite comes in small packages!

SMALLEST EYE—EYE CAN'T SEE YOU!

Wow! I barely can see you!

That's what I thought when I was looking at satellite loops, searching for the eye of Hurricane Wilma! Wilma's eye was only 2 miles in diameter when she was at her strongest, on October 19, 2005, in the Caribbean.

Wilma also owns the record for the strongest hurricane in the Atlantic basin with that record low pressure of 882 mb! Wilma may have been small, but just ask anyone in Florida and they will tell you, she packed a wallop!

WHO'S THE BIGGEST, BADDEST, AND MEANEST OUT THERE?

Super Typhoon Tip! No question!

DEADLIEST EVER!

The deadliest tropical storm that ever occurred was in the Brahmaputra River Delta of Bangladesh on November 12, 1970. A storm surge of 40 feet (five stories high on a building and one of the highest ever recorded!) flooded the islands at the head of the Bay of Bengal. The islands are densely populated and, unfortunately, an estimated 300,000 to 500,000 lives were lost.

WHAT'S THE HURRY? WHO'S THE FASTEST?

In the Atlantic, Hurricane Humberto is the big winner! Just off the coast of Texas in 2007, Humberto set a speed record for intensification. In just 14 hours 15 minutes, it went from a tropical depression to a full-blown hurricane.

Super Typhoon Forrest, cruising in the western Pacific during September 1983, saw his wind strength go from 75 mph to 175 mph in just 24 hours. Wow!

WHOA—TOO MUCH COFFEE, WAY TOO INTENSE!

Hurricane Wilma is the most powerful storm ever observed in the Western Hemisphere. On October 19, 2005, its record low pressure of 26.04 inches of mercury was observed south of

Cuba. Wilma's maximum sustained winds reached 185 mph.

Thank goodness Wilma never hit land with her full force!

Hurricane Katrina's eyewall as seen by the Hurricane Hunters

WHAT HURRICANE HAS COST THE MOST?

Hurricane Katrina is currently the costliest hurricane in U.S. history. Crashing through Alabama, Florida, Louisiana, and Mississippi in August 2005, Katrina's total bill has been estimated at $100 billion.

The entire cost may never be known as it may take several generations for New Orleans to return to what it was. Katrina's losses went beyond money. As

many as 1,836 people died as a result of the storm, making it one of the most deadly hurricanes in recorded history.

DEADLIEST HURRICANE OF THE ATLANTIC BASIN

At the end of the Era of the Pirates, the Great Hurricane of 1780 swept through Barbados, St. Vincent, Martinique, Dominica, Guadaloupe, and St. Lucia. It's not on any list because the actual numbers cannot be confirmed, but it's believed to have killed some 22,000 sailors, pirates, and townspeople, as well as nearly wiping out the entire British navy! Wonder where Captain Jack Sparrow was? Barbarossa?

WHO'S THE MOST POWERFUL IN THE EASTERN PACIFIC?

Hurricane Linda formed off the west coast of Mexico in 1997. Her wind speeds reached 185 mph with 220 mph gusts.

Linda can thank El Niño for her power. It was a very strong El Niño season that year; during 1997–1998, five of the strongest Pacific typhoons on record developed.

El Niño is present when there is a relaxing of the trade winds in the western Pacific. When that happens (we don't know why it does), El Niño brings warm water from the western Pacific to the eastern Pacific . . . and what simple ingredient do we need to make a strong hurricane?

Right! Warm water!

Fortunately, Hurricane Linda never made landfall. She headed north and dissolved into the great beyond!.

WHAT SEASON HAS THE HIGHEST BATTING AVERAGE?

The hurricane season of 2005 was certainly extreme! There were so many storms that we ran out of names! The National Hurricane Center had to turn to the Greek alphabet to name storms—there were Alpha, Beta, Gamma, Delta, Epsilon, and Zeta.

Altogether, twenty-eight tropical storms formed, producing fifteen hurricanes—which also was a record.

WHAT SEASON HAS THE LOWEST BATTING AVERAGE?

Only one storm made it to the plate in 1890 and 1914. There must have been really good pitching.

THE BASES ARE LOADED!

Back on August 22, 1893, four raging hurricanes were cruising through the Atlantic Ocean.

One of those storms, which on August 22 was located between the Bahamas and Bermuda, went on to hit New York City!

Two storms were near the Cape Verde islands off the African coast, and a fourth was approaching Nova Scotia.

The Cape Verde storms eventually came ashore over Georgia and South Carolina on August 27, killing as many as 2,000 people.

Meteorologists really needed a scorecard to keep track of these!

HEY! YOU MUST BE IN THE WITNESS PROTECTION PROGRAM!

What's in a name? One hurricane had three names! Imagine a storm crossing from the Gulf of Mexico to the Pacific and back again. . . .

In the name game we have—of naming storms different names in different oceans—you knew this was bound to happen some day. If a storm crosses from one ocean to another, say from the Atlantic to the Pacific, the name of the storm changes from an Atlantic name to a Pacific name. And vice versa.

Tropical Storm Hattie developed on October 28, 1961, off the Caribbean coast of Nicaragua. After crossing Central America, the storm re-formed in the Pacific Ocean, where she was given the name Simone on November 1. Two days later, she curled back toward Central America, crossing back to the Atlantic through Mexico and reemerged in the Gulf of Mexico as Inga!

I hope she got frequent flier miles!

Living Through Hurricane Camille— or, How I Came to Be a Meteorologist

I grew up in the 1960s (I know that's a long time ago; some people think I used to forecast the weather for President George Washington!). It was a wild and sometimes frightening time. There were race riots, war, assassinations, environmental disasters, and even the god-awful threat of nuclear weapons being used, all beamed by television right into our living rooms.

I grew up in the rural South where, during this time, communities did their best to sort of cut themselves off from this tumultuous time in our nation's history. Soon that came to an abrupt and horrifying end.

As a nine-year-old boy in August of 1969, I personally had a front-row seat to see a disastrous monster of a hurricane named Camille shock our state right out of its isolation with the most powerful hurricane to strike the U.S. mainland in recorded history. Camille's winds, at the time, were clocked at 174 mph with winds as high as 201 mph extrapolated by the Hurricane Hunter aircraft from above. Her storm surge, reaching more than 28 feet, also set a record.

As the storm approached the Mississippi Gulf Coast from the central Gulf of Mexico, I kept a homemade hurricane tracking chart.

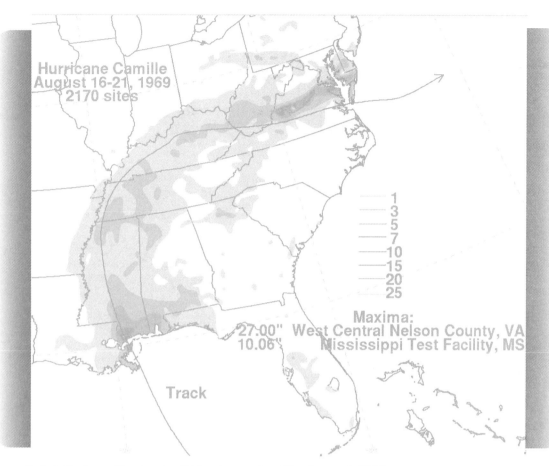

Hurricane Camille
August 16-21, 1969
2170 sites

1
3
5
7
10
15
20
25

Maxima:
27.00" West Central Nelson County, VA
10.06" Mississippi Test Facility, MS

Track

Rainfall along the track of Hurricane Camille, August 1969

It was a Texaco road map of the southeastern United States that showed just enough of the Gulf of Mexico to give me room to write in Camille's position. Listening to the radio and watching the weather reports on TV, I wrote down the longitude and latitude from each report. Camille clipped the far western tip of Cuba to the middle of the Gulf of Mexico, coming ashore just east of Biloxi, Mississippi.

Advisories like this were issued:

ADVISORY NO. 2 6 PM EDT THURSDAY AUGUST 14, 1969

. . . YOUNG CAMILLE ADVANCES SLOWLY TOWARD THE GULF OF MEXICO . . .

NO FURTHER REPORTS HAVE BEEN RECEIVED FROM THE DEVELOPING CENTRAL AREAS OF CAMILLE DURING THE AFTERNOON AND BOTH THE MOVEMENT AND PRESENT INTENSITY MUST BE INFERRED FROM ISLAND STATION REPORTS. AT 6 PM EDT . . . 2200Z . . . CAMILLE WAS LOCATED APPROXIMATELY AT LATITUDE 19.9 NORTH . . . LONGITUDE 83.0 WEST OR ABOUT 440 MILES SOUTH SOUTHWEST OF MIAMI. IT IS APPARENTLY MOVING NORTHWEST ABOUT 12 MPH. BASED UPON THE ESSA 9 SATELLITE PICTURE JUST RECEIVED THE STORM HAS NOT SIGNIFICANTLY INCREASED IN INTENSITY DURING THE LAST 6 HOURS AND STRONGEST WINDS ARE ESTIMATED TO BE 60 TO 65 MPH OVER A SMALL AREA NEAR THE CENTER. GALES EXTEND OUTWARD 70 TO 100 MILES IN THE NORTHERN SEMICIRCLE OF THE STORM.

INDICATIONS ARE THAT CAMILLE WILL PASS NEAR THE WESTERN TIP OF CUBA TONIGHT OR EARLY FRIDAY MORNING MOVING NORTHWESTWARD ABOUT 10 TO 12 MPH. WHILE IT IS TOO EARLY TO DETERMINE WHAT FURTHER LAND AREAS MAY BE AFFECTED BY THIS STORM THE STEERING CURRENTS INDICATE THE LIKELIHOOD OF A TURN TO A SLIGHTLY MORE NORTHERLY COURSE FRIDAY. THIS WOULD CARRY THE CENTER INTO THE EAST CENTRAL GULF OF MEXICO THIS WEEKEND.

ALL INTERESTS IN THE FLORIDA KEYS AND SHIPPING IN THE VICINITY OF THE YUCATAN CHANNEL AND THE EASTERN GULF OF MEXICO SHOULD REMAIN ALERT FOR FURTHER ADVICES CONCERNING THE DEVELOPMENT AND MOVEMENT OF CAMILLE. WHILE THIS IS A VERY SMALL STORM AT PRESENT . . . CONDITIONS ARE FAVORABLE FOR FURTHER DEVELOPMENT.

ALL INTERESTS IN WESTERN CUBA SHOULD BE PREPARED FOR WINDS OF GALE FORCE IN SQUALLS AND THE POSSIBILITY OF HEAVY RAINS AND FLASH FLOODS TONIGHT WITH TIDES ALONG THE SOUTHWEST COASTLINE 3 TO 5 FEET ABOVE NORMAL.

REPEATING THE 6 PM EDT POSITION . . . 19.9 NORTH . . . 83.0 WEST.

THE NEXT ADVISORY WILL BE ISSUED BY THE NATIONAL HURRICANE CENTER AT MIDNIGHT EDT.

SIMPSON*

---

*Yes, that's right, the Simpson who wrote the advisory is the same person who helped invent the Saffir-Simpson Scale!

As Camille roared ashore in the middle of the night over the Mississippi Gulf Coast with all its ferociousness, I kept up with the reports, even when the power went out—I had a battery-operated AM radio and a citizens band (CB) radio. The winds battered our home to the point where my grandfather moved the refrigerator behind the door to our home to keep it from blowing in.

Camille's winds destroyed the roof of our home, and our beautiful pecan orchard was stripped bare of every pecan and every single leaf. The winds made this eerie, moaning, deathlike sound like right out of a horror movie. Imagine what it must have been like to live through this at only nine years old. The numbers came in: 172 Mississippians were killed by Camille; 41 were never found, presumed washed out to sea. The national death toll was 347. Camille destroyed Plaquemines Parish, Louisiana, and dumped 32 inches of rain over Virginia, causing 150 mudslides.

Today, there are still bare concrete slabs, vestiges from Camille's wrath dotting the Mississippi coastline. In her wake, Camille left a wave of change for the better in the way the United States deals with hurricane disasters. Camille's legacy includes improvements in emergency

management planning; the creation of the Federal Emergency Management Agency (FEMA); and increased support for scientific and engineering research, resulting in new building codes and the Saffir-Simpson Damage-Potential Scale, as well as better understanding of the psychological effects of disaster trauma.

Speaking of psychological trauma, here are two bizarre stories from Camille. The first is the story of how Camille got her name.

Before the creation of the World Meteorological Organization (WMO), which names hurricanes, storms were named by the meteorologists in the National Hurricane Center in Coral Gables, Florida. Early in 1969, one of the forecasters placed his daughter's name on the list for the upcoming hurricane season: Camille.

This is the only case known where a real live person's name was placed on the list of hurricane names. Camille the person is still around today, living with the distinction of having lent her name to one of the most destructive hurricanes in history. Camille the hurricane had her name retired. There will never again be a Hurricane Camille.

The next story is about the saucy cocktail waitress from Pass Christian, Mississippi, named Mary Ann Gerlach. She lived at the Richelieu Apartments complex, where twenty-three people had a hurricane party just before Camille made landfall. The Richelieu was a civil defense shelter, meaning the building should have been strong enough to remain standing in the event of nuclear war.

Well, it wasn't. As the hurricane party took place, on the third floor, Camille's storm surge washed the entire complex from its foundation. Mary Ann Gerlach was swept out of the building by the water. She managed to cling to a tree about half a mile inland by the railroad tracks in town. She claimed to be the only survivor of the festivity; even her husband was killed in the storm surge. However, two others from the Richelieu also survived . . . and they say the party never happened.

I've interviewed Mary Ann and I can tell you, with her sweet Southern accent, she was quite a storyteller. She also went on to have eleven (that's right, *eleven*) husbands.

Mary Ann had a dark side. Ten years after Camille, Mary Ann killed one of her husbands. She said her actions were due to the post-traumatic stress she had endured while clinging for her life to a tree during Hurricane Camille. Whoa, cue the *Twilight Zone* music! She was quite a character.

The Richelieu Apartments complex before Camille

The Richelieu Apartments complex after Camille

But Mary Ann Gerlach wasn't the only character in the story of Camille. My favorite is the hero weatherman from New Orleans, Nash Roberts.

Nash was his own guy. He didn't rely on the National Hurricane Center's forecasts. He did his own forecast and predicted the path of Camille so accurately that it was eerie! Nash Roberts is the most beloved weatherman in the history of New Orleans.

Lots of folks like to compare 2005's Hurricane Katrina to 1969's Hurricane Camille because of their similar strengths and nearly identical landfall locations. Before Katrina, Camille was considered to be the benchmark against which all Gulf Coast hurricanes were measured. Katrina was weaker than Camille at landfall but was substantially larger, which led to both a broader and a larger storm surge. Katrina was described by those who had also experienced Camille as "much worse"— not only because of the massive storm surge, but because Katrina pounded the Mississippi coast for a longer period of time.

Camille also drew part of its record storm surge from adjacent coastal waters; Lake Borgne and Lake Pontchartrain actually receded, sparing some of the city of New Orleans from flooding.

Katrina's death toll was made slightly higher because those who survived Camille—with no flooding and little damage—believed Katrina to be a less serious threat. This false sense of security among Camille veterans accounted for as many as 7 percent of those who chose not to evacuate. An innkeeper at the Harbour Oaks Inn, Tony Brugger, was killed when his inn collapsed.

Before 1969, many residents of the Gulf Coast had weathered the effects of Hurricane Betsy, a strong, Category 3 hurricane that had made landfall in 1965. Betsy, up until that point, had been the benchmark for Gulf hurricanes and many people ignored the warnings for Camille, believing that a hurricane could not get any stronger. Unfortunately, when Katrina hit, the same mentality persisted, and those who survived Camille felt that they could survive Katrina and thus did not evacuate.

You should always have a plan for when a storm like Camille or Katrina is coming. Almost always, if you live on the water, you will have to evacuate. Make a plan. Make it today, because when the storm is coming, it's already too late.

Trinity Episcopalian Church before Camille

Where Will the Next Big Storm Strike? Could There Be Another Katrina?

I write this section not to scare the people I am about to talk about, but to make them aware, so they can be prepared. I, along with Marianna Jameson, wrote a thriller called *Category 7*. It's a great story, which you should read. It's about an evil guy who figures out how to create and manipulate weather. In a psychotic rage, he creates a hurricane and points it toward a particular city: New York City.

I wrote the book not only to entertain, but also to make people aware of the vulnerability of the New York City area to a major Category 3 hurricane striking and creating catastrophic devastation to life and property.

There are two different and important parts of meteorology. There's weather, and there's what's called *climatology*. Weather is what's going on outside right now. Climatology is weather that has

Trinity Episcopalian Church after Camille

taken place over a number of years, decades, or centuries.

Climatology shows us that weather events like hurricanes repeat over and over in certain areas. The number of years between events may be shorter or longer, depending on where they take place.

Let's take tornadoes. If you live in Oklahoma, you know that every one out of two years, you are going to be involved with a tornado. But if you live in Brooklyn, New York, a tornado like the EF1 funnel cloud that touched down in 2007 is a surprise—because the last time a tornado appeared in Brooklyn was in 1907, a hundred years earlier.

Obviously, tornadoes happen more frequently in Oklahoma than in New York, but the history of weather shows us that though it might be a hundred years before you see one, tornadoes do happen in Brooklyn, New York.

The next job of climatology is to teach us about frequency: How much time goes by before a hurricane strikes a particular area? If you live on the U.S. Gulf Coast, that frequency is more often than if you live in the mid-Atlantic or the Northeast. But just because hurricanes strike less often in the mid-Atlantic or the Northeast doesn't mean they won't strike again.

Climatology teaches us that there may be a gap of many years between storms, but they have happened and they will happen again. Weather repeats itself.

What does climatology teach us about hurricanes in the Northeast? It tells us that every 70 years a major hurricane strikes the region. The last storm was the hurricane of 1938, called the Long Island Express. This Category 3 storm had winds of 121 mph when it made landfall in Suffolk County, Long Island, New York. Blue Hill Observatory in Massachusetts recorded a wind speed of 186 mph. The previous storm of that size had taken place in 1869, nearly 70 years before. You can see that climatology shows that every 70 years, a major hurricane of Category 3 strength strikes the New York City area.

Hurricanes in the Northeast are totally different animals from hurricanes in the South. Where a storm has an average forward speed of 8 to 14 mph in the southeast United States, a storm in the Northeast has a forward speed averaging 45 mph. The Long Island Express had a forward speed of 70 mph due to the Gulf Stream, the powerful, warm, and swift ocean current that runs south to north from the Florida Keys to Newfoundland and across the Atlantic.

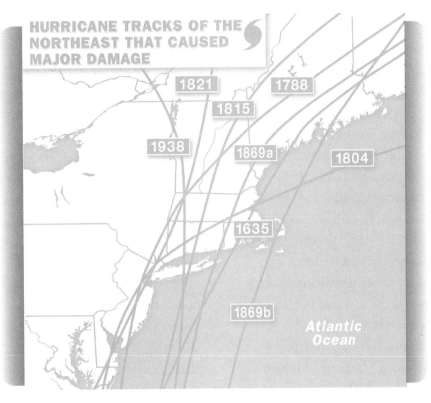

HURRICANE TRACKS OF THE NORTHEAST THAT CAUSED MAJOR DAMAGE

1821
1788
1815
1938
1869a
1804
1635
1869b
Atlantic Ocean

The eye of the storm was 55 miles in diameter. This huge storm caused tremendous devastation in New York, Connecticut, Rhode Island, and Massachusetts, as well as Vermont and New Hampshire. A single meteorologist, Charlie Pierce, at the time a junior forecaster working for what was then called the Weather Bureau, predicted that the storm would head straight north to New York. His warning never went out because he was overruled by the chief forecaster, who believed the hurricane would curve out into the Atlantic as most storms do.

Thus the Long Island Express was the greatest unforeseen natural disaster in the history of Long Island. It caught everyone by surprise and hit at high tide to boot. The storm surge averaged 18 feet on the eastern end of Long Island, and 50 feet in Massachusetts. The hurricane killed 682 people. The damage was all due to the storm surge and wind. The storm's fast-forward movement did not allow for a huge amount of rain, so there was minimal inland flooding.

At a cinema in Westhampton, Long Island, the surge carried twenty people at a matinee out to sea. It carried the theater, projectionist and all, 2 miles out into the Atlantic where they drowned. The storm destroyed two billion trees throughout New England. You can go to Vermont today and still see where trees were destroyed by the 1938 storm.

The New York City area has a history of being ravaged by hurricanes. Talk about bizarre—the only known incident of a hurricane wiping out a whole island happened in New York City. Hog Island, originally used by the Indians to raise pigs and later developed with casinos and bath houses, lay just to the south of Long Island. In the middle of the night on August 23, 1893, a Category 2 storm washed Hog Island from the face of the earth and erased it from every map.

What makes New York City so vulnerable?

Geography and geology. The landmass from New Jersey to New York City to Long Island creates a right angle. There are only three right-angle landmasses where hurricanes strike. Northwest Florida, New York, and New Orleans all have right-angle landmasses. Research Katrina and you'll see how devastating that can be.

Hurricane winds move in a counterclockwise rotation. The storm surge pours water right to left into that right-angle landmass. The water has nowhere to go except inland.

The other factor, geology, has to do with the bottom of the Atlantic. In

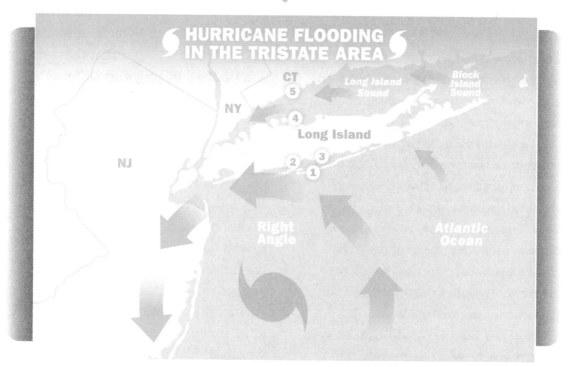

The numbers indicate the five most densely populated coastal areas in the United States.

the southern United States, the bottom of the Gulf of Mexico is sand, which absorbs a good deal of the energy a hurricane forces into the water. In the northeast, the sea floor is a stone called *schist*, which absorbs nothing. The hurricane forces energy into the ocean and every bit of this energy is forced upward and onto land.

This causes the storm surge to be worse in a northeastern storm. In terms of storm surge, the geography and geology combine to make a Category 1 storm actually a Category 2, a Category 2 becomes a 3 in terms of storm surge, and so on. A northeastern hurricane is very different from, and can be more dangerous than, a Gulf storm.

There are other factors that make New York City the most vulnerable city on Earth for catastrophic devastation from a hurricane.

Everything that is vital to life in New York City sits on the water. It's easy sometimes to forget that New York is a port city, but it is, and it's surrounded by water. Waste water treatment plants, coal and garbage-burning electrical power plants, a nuclear power plant, military bases, police and fire stations: all the major infrastructure sits on water. It's the most densely populated stretch of coastline in the country.

Airports like JFK and La Guardia, which did not exist at the time of the 1938 storm, now rest beside the waters of Flushing Bay and Jamaica Bay.

It's all a recipe for disaster.

Just look at the population of Long Island alone. In 1938, there were just 200,000 residents; today there are two million. Add in the summer tourists and you have nearly three million people inhabiting a long, skinny island with few access routes. The East End, where all the "beautiful" people go in August, has only *one* road out! The loss of life during a major hurricane on Long Island might eclipse the 1,836 lives lost in New Orleans during Hurricane Katrina.

I see two great problems for New York City.

The first is lack of experience. Residents have to go back 70 years to recall such a great storm and that is a very long time. Most of the people living in New York now had not yet been born or had moved to the city long after 1938. Generations go by without the experience of dealing with a monstrous Category 3 hurricane. Many people believe that hurricanes of that nature never strike New York. Even at the time, the city was unaware of what it was in for. The main headline of *The New York*

Times that day read NEVILLE CHAMBERLAIN TO MEET WITH HITLER.

Not long ago, I took a TV crew and went out on the streets of New York City to do a story for a hurricane documentary we were doing. I asked residents where they would go if a hurricane was about to strike the city. The answer I got was astounding. The overwhelming majority answered that they would seek refuge from a Category 3 hurricane by going down into the subway, where they would inevitably be drowned by the storm surge.

Amazing as this might seem, it's not too surprising when you realize that many inner-city residents have spent their lives seeking shelter from blizzards, nor'easters, and extreme cold by utilizing the subway.

The second problem is apathy—the generally held belief that a Category 3 storm will never hit the New York City area. And if it does, New Yorkers feel they will be able to go about their day and just deal with it. It's a syndrome I call "I'm a New Yorker, and I gargle nails for breakfast!" New Yorkers

are a tough breed, no doubt, but while they can shovel 30 inches of snow, no one can shovel the ocean.

The devastation will be tremendous and catastrophic, to say the very least. Salt water from the Atlantic will pour into the subway system, killing it. The same ocean will destroy the underground communications systems for the largest and most important financial center in the world, Wall Street. A Category 3 storm will produce a storm surge of nearly 30 feet, higher if the storm arrives at high tide. That would put water in the streets up to midtown Manhattan. The water might reach a height of three stories on the buildings around lower Manhattan, in the area called the Battery and Wall Street.

As the storm leaves, its winds would shift to the northeast, flooding the city from the north. Though the storm will move quickly, racing by at 45 mph, its devastation in this densely populated area would be extreme. It has the smell and feel of another Hurricane Katrina.

New York City officials are well aware of this threat, but as I said, few have experience with such a monster. Officials have a plan that will involve evacuating the three million people who live in the most storm-vulnerable parts of the city. These will not exactly be three million happy-go-lucky-whistling-a-tune evacuees. They will be three million panicked people without a clue of what to expect. I guess that many New Yorkers who live right on the water, the "I gargle nails for breakfast" crowd, will not leave—like so many who tried to outlast Katrina in New Orleans.

My nephew Nathan, a sergeant in the National Guard, said that in all his service to our country, in war and peace, he had never seen anything like the situation during the flooding of New Orleans. He actually had to draw his weapon to defend himself from a fellow U.S. citizen whom he was trying to get to leave a flooded home. The flood waters had risen to the roof of the home; he and his fellow soldiers had cut a hole in the roof to help the residents escape from the attic. The guardsmen were attacked by people armed with knives—people who apparently would rather drown in their home than be evacuated. Stranger things will happen in New York City. There's way more people living there.

My point in all of this is to say that people should have a plan of action for when the storm comes.

Notice I did not say *if* the storm comes.

Climatology shows that hurricanes hit New York City. There just may be a long period of time in between.

It has happened before and it will happen again.

Great Hurricane Web Sites >>>>

www.aoml.noaa.gov/hrd/tcfaq/tcfaqHED.html

www.2010.atmos.uiuc.edu/(Gh)/guides/mtr/hurr/stages/cane/home.rxml

www.nasa.gov/worldbook/hurricane_worldbook.html

http://teachertech.rice.edu/Participants/louviere/hurricanes/stages.html

www.weatherwizkids.com/hurricane1.html

Try This at Home!

Let's Make It Rain!

This is from the Weather Wiz Kids Web site (www. weatherwizkids.com). Since we've been talking about hurricanes in this chapter, let's see how moisture condenses to make rain!

MATERIALS:

Glass mayonnaise
   or canning jar
Plate (not a paper plate)
Very hot water
Ice cubes
Index cards

PROCESS:

Pour about two inches of very hot water into the glass jar.

Cover the jar with the plate and wait a few minutes before you perform the next step.

Put the ice cubes on top of the plate.

EXPLANATION:

What happens? The cold plate causes the moisture in the warm air inside the jar to condense and form water droplets. This is the same thing that happens in the atmosphere. Warm, moist air rises and meets colder air high in the atmosphere. The water vapor condenses and forms precipitation that falls to the ground.

SECTION

3

BLIZZARDS

How Bizarre! Blizzards, Snowstorms, and Ice, Oh My!

Blizzards are the worst weather that winter can dish out! Whenever you hear someone exclaim, "It looks like a blizzard outside!" they're generally talking about the nastiest of days. Meteorologists and weather forecasters use the term blizzard to describe a day of heavy snow, biting winds, and low visibility. The term *blizzard* originally meant a cannon shot or a volley of musket fire until an Iowa newspaper used the term in 1870 to describe a snowstorm. Blizzards can occur in any location in the world where snow is naturally made.

What Makes a Snowstorm a Blizzard?

Officially, the National Weather Service defines a blizzard as a storm that contains large amounts of snow *or* blowing snow, has winds in excess of 35 mph and visibilities of less than a quarter mile, and lasts for at least 3 hours. When these conditions are expected, the National Weather Service will issue a blizzard warning. Blizzard conditions often develop on the northwest side of an intense storm system. The difference between the lower pressure in the storm and the higher pressure to the west creates a tight pressure gradient, or difference in pressure between two locations, which in turn results in very strong winds. These strong winds pick up any available snow from the ground, and/or blow about any snow which is falling, creating very low visibility and the potential for significant drifting of snow.

Cold polar air that whips freshly fallen, fine, powdery snow off the ground creates what is called a *ground blizzard*.

Blizzards can create life-threatening conditions. Traveling by automobile can become difficult, or even impossible, due to whiteout conditions and drifting snow. Whiteout conditions are most often caused by major storms that produce a dry, very powdery snow. In this situation, it doesn't even need to be snowing for there to be a whiteout. When the snow that is already on the ground is blown around, visibility can be reduced to near zero at times.

During a blizzard, gusty winds can knock down trees, bringing down power lines and cutting off electricity for extended periods of time. Often, it can be snowing so hard, at the rate of 2 to 4 inches per hour, that thunder can be heard and flashes of lightning seen. When that happens, it's called *thundersnow*. The conditions for making thundersnow are the same as in a thunderstorm except the precipitation falls in the form of snow rather than rain. It's a very rare phenomenon that happens when very cold air slams into warm air, along a cold or warm front, or a strong storm system that has a very strong upward motion of wind.

How Do You Make That Snowy Stuff?

To me, snow is by far the most beautiful of all of the various forms of precipitation. To put it simply, snow is cool! The way snow is made is really complex . . . and some parts of the process still remain a mystery. Snowflakes are made from the water droplets in a cloud, just like rain. But in winter, the water vapor is *supercooled*—cooled below freezing and frozen into ice crystals. That happens around 14°F (-10°C). Snowflakes are made from ice crystals, pure and simple. Sure, rain can freeze, but frozen rain is called *sleet* and it's structurally very different from snow.

Do you know that most snowflakes have six sides? Do you know why? The water molecules in ice crystals form a hexagonal lattice—that is, they have six sides––so when a water droplet freezes, it forms the six-fold symmetry of snow crystals. The most basic snowflake shape is known as a hexagonal prism.

The word *snowflake* is a general term for many ice crystals that have come together. A snowflake can be made up of two crystals or hundreds. A flake's six beautiful points are determined by the amount of ice crystals and the temperature of the atmosphere.

Snowflakes are mysterious things. Their sides and points are symmetrical, and their fundamental form derives from the arrangement of the water molecules in the ice crystal. When a liquid freezes, the molecules tend to settle in the lowest-energy state, and that almost

always involves some form of symmetry. The higher the symmetry, the more stable the crystal is.

Dendrite snowflake

Water molecules floating freely in a vapor begin to arrange themselves into a crystalline solid when the temperature drops below freezing. The two hydrogen atoms of the molecules tend to attract neighboring water molecules. When

the temperature is low enough, the molecules link together to form a solid, open framework that has a strict hexagonal symmetry.

Why are snowflake shapes so elaborate? Nobody has a good answer for that. The general explanation is that atmospheric conditions when snowflakes are forming are very complex and variable. A crystal might begin to grow in one manner and then minutes or even seconds later, something changes (temperature or humidity), so it starts to grow in another manner. The hexagonal symmetry is maintained, but the ice crystal may branch off in new directions.

These changes in environment take place over a large area compared with the size of a single snowflake, so all the flakes developing in the same region are similarly affected. In the end, all kinds of forms can arise: everything from prisms and needles to the familiar lacy snowflakes. Water is an amazing substance!

The Life of a Snowflake

The shape and size of snow crystals depend on the amount of water

vapor in the air and the temperature of the atmosphere. Crystals take on different shapes depending on the amount of time they spend blowing around in the snow cloud and what the overall weather conditions are.

Snow Morphology

There are all kinds of snowflakes, many more types than most of us may have ever thought existed. The amount of moisture and the temperature of the air determine the size and shape of snowflakes. Some flakes are very fine and some are as big as pancakes.

Thin plates and stars grow around 28°F (-2°C), while columns and slender needles appear near 23°F (-5°C). Plates and stars again form near 5°F (-15°C), and a combination of plates and columns are made around -22°F (-30°C).

Snow crystals tend to form simpler shapes when the humidity is low, while more complex shapes form at higher humidities. The most extreme shapes—long needles around 23°F (-5°C) and large, thin plates around -5°F (-15°C)—form when the humidity is especially high. Why snow crystal shapes change so much with temperature remains something of a scientific mystery. The growth of snowflakes depends on exactly how water vapor molecules are incorporated into the developing ice crystal, and the physics behind this is complex and not well understood. Most snowflakes are irregular and perfect ones are rare. Next time you are wearing gloves and it's snowing, take a good look at the flakes in your hand. What are they? Are they plates, stars, or needles? Better yet, if you can, get a look at them under a microscope and you'll see that no two snowflakes are alike.

Some people think that "No two snowflakes are alike" is just a folk saying, but it is a true statement and there are many reasons for it. The size and shape of snowflakes are influenced by many things: air currents (which direction the air is moving), humidity levels (the amount of water vapor in the air), wind speed, pressure from the weight of other crystals, the combination of one snow crystal with another, and how long it takes the crystal to fall. There is an infinite variety of snowflakes. You can spend your whole life looking at snowflakes and never find two that are alike!

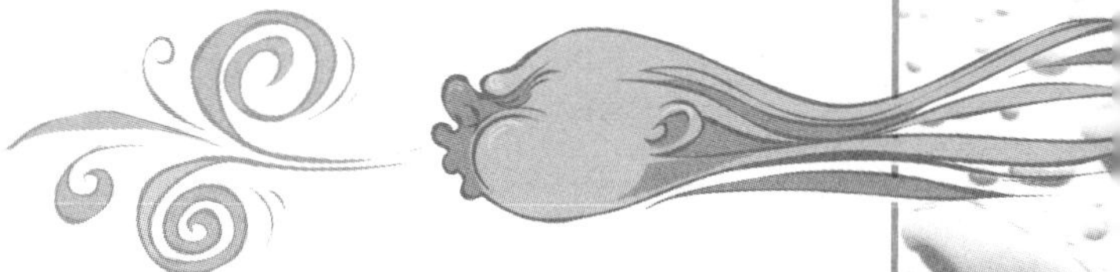

Types of Snowflakes

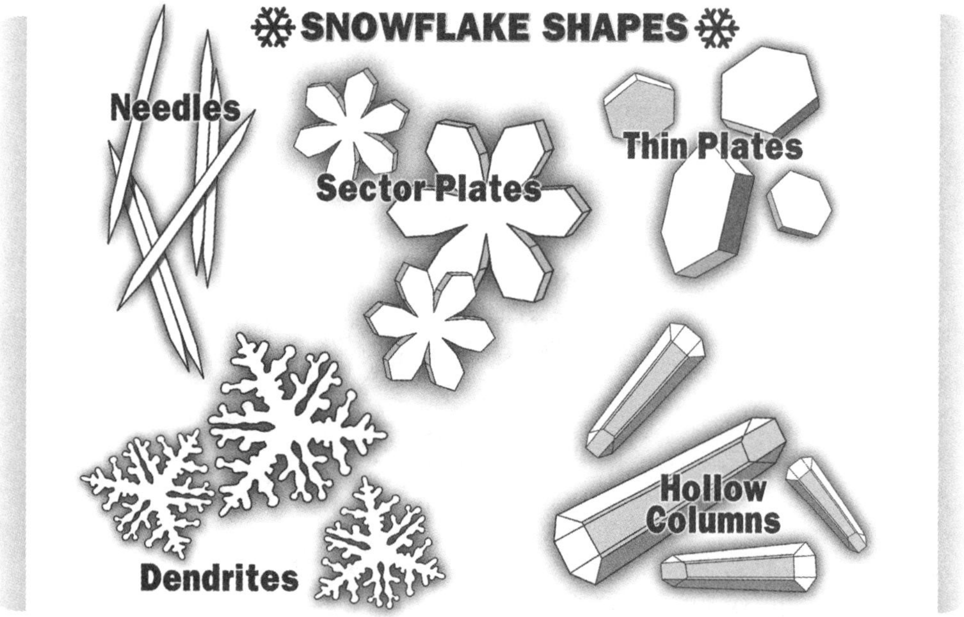

❄ SNOWFLAKE SHAPES ❄

Needles

Sector Plates

Thin Plates

Dendrites

Hollow Columns

Simple Prisms

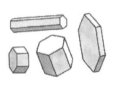

A hexagonal prism is the most basic snow crystal. Depending on how fast the different facets grow, snow crystal prisms can appear as thin hexagonal plates, slender hexagonal columns (shaped a lot like wooden pencils), or anything in between. Simple prisms are usually so small they can barely be seen with the naked eye.

The examples at right show two stubby prisms (left and right) and one thin plate (center). Snow crystal facets are rarely perfectly flat, being more typically decorated with various indents, ridges, or other features.

Stellar Plates

These common snowflakes are thin, platelike crystals with six broad arms that form a starlike shape. Their faces are often decorated with amazingly elaborate and symmetrical markings.

Platelike snowflakes form when the temperature is near 28°F (-2° C) or near 5°F (-15°C).

Sectored Plates

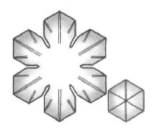

Stellar plates often show distinctive ridges that point to the corners between adjacent prism facets. When these ridges are especially prominent, the crystals are called sectored plates.

The simplest sectored plates are hexagonal crystals that are divided into six equal pieces, like the slices of a hexagonal pie. More complex specimens show prominent ridges on broad, flat branches.

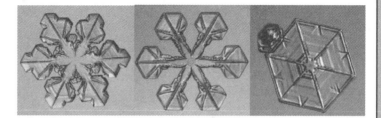

Stellar Dendrites

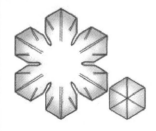

Dendritic means treelike, so stellar dendrites are platelike snow crystals that have branches, and sometimes, side branches. These are fairly large crystals, typically 2 to 4 mm in diameter, that can be easily seen with the naked eye.

Judging by holiday and winter decorations, stellar dendrites are the most popular type of snow crystal. You can see these crystals for yourself quite well with just a simple magnifier.

Fernlike Stellar Dendrites

Sometimes the branches of stellar crystals have so many side branches they look a bit like ferns, so we call them fernlike stellar dendrites. These are the largest snow crystals, often 5 mm or more in diameter. In spite of their large size, these are single crystals of ice—the water molecules are lined up from one end to the other.

Some snowfalls contain almost nothing but stellar dendrites and fernlike stellar dendrites. It's quite a sight when they collect in vast numbers, blanketing everything in white.

The best powder snow, where you sink to your knees while skiing, is made of stellar dendrites. These crystals can be extremely thin and light, so they make a low-density snowpack.

Hollow Columns

When hexagonal columns form with hollow conical regions at each end, such forms are called hollow columns. These crystals are small, so you need a good magnifier to see the hollow regions. Columns form near 23°F (−5°C), and near −22°F (−30°C).

Note how the two hollow regions are symmetrical in each column. Sometimes the ends grow over and enclose a pair of bubbles in the ice.

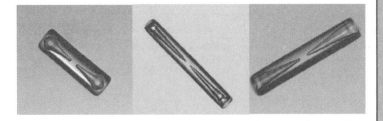

Needles

Needles are slender, columnar ice crystals that grow when the temperature is around 23°F (-5°C). On your sleeve these snowflakes look like small bits of white hair.

A shift of just a few degrees in temperature changes the pattern of crystal growth from thin, flat plates to long, slender needles. Why this happens is still unknown.

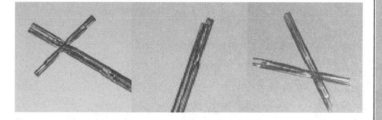

Capped Columns

These crystals first grow as stubby columns which are blown into a region of the clouds where conditions cause crystals to grow into plates. The result is two thin, platelike crystals growing on the ends of an ice column. Capped columns don't appear in every snowfall, but you can find them if you look for them.

The three small illustrations at the right are three views of a capped column. The top view is from the side, showing the central column and the two plates edge-on. The other two views show the same crystal from one end, with the microscope focused separately on each of the two plates. The other three images are also of capped columns from the side.

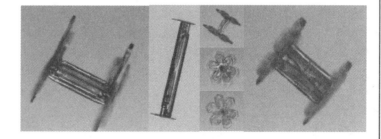

Double Plates

A double plate is basically a capped column with an especially short central column. One plate grows more quickly than the other, and because the two plates are so close together, the larger one shields the smaller from some water vapor. These crystals are common—many snowflakes that look like ordinary stellar plates are actually double plates if you look closely.

The picture at the far right shows a double plate from the side. The center picture shows a double plate with the microscope focused on the smaller plate. In the picture on the left, note the slightly out-of-focus hexagon that is about one-sixth as large as the main crystal. This hexagon is the second side of a double plate, connected to the main plate by a small axle.

Split Plates and Stars

These are forms of double plates, except that part of one plate grows large along with part of the other plate. Split plates and stars, like double plates, are common but often go unnoticed.

You may have to stare at these pictures a bit to see how the two distinct pieces fit together. Note how in each case the crystals are connected in the center with short axles.

Triangular Crystals

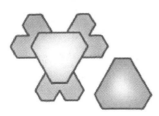

Plates sometimes grow as truncated triangles when the temperature is near 28°F (2°C). If the corners of the plates sprout arms, the result is an odd version of a stellar plate crystal. These crystals are relatively rare.

Surprisingly, no one knows why snow crystals grow into these three-fold symmetrical shapes. (Note, however, that the molecular structure of triangular crystals is no different from ordinary six-sided crystals. The facet angles are all the same.)

12-Sided Snowflakes

Sometimes capped columns form with a twist, a 30-degree twist to be specific. The two end-plates are both six-branched crystals, but one is rotated 30 degrees relative to the other. This is a form of crystal *twinning*, in which two crystals grow joined in a specific orientation.

These crystals are very rare, but sometimes a snowfall will bring quite a few. The picture in the center shows a 12-sider where the two halves are widely separated.

Bullet Rosettes

The nucleation of an ice grain sometimes yields multiple linked crystals that grow together at random orientations. When the different pieces grow into columns, the result is called a *bullet rosette*. These polycrystals often break up into isolated bullet-shaped crystals.

Sometimes a bullet rosette can become a capped rosette, as shown in the example in the middle.

Radiating Dendrites

When the pieces of a polycrystal grow out into dendrites, the result is called a *radiating dendrite* or a *spatial dendrite*.

The far example on the right shows radiating plates. The other example shows a fernlike stellar dendrite with two errant branches growing up out of the main plane of the crystal.

Rimed Crystals

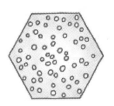

Clouds are made of countless water droplets, and sometimes these droplets collide with and stick to snow crystals. The frozen droplets are called *rime*. All the different types of snow crystals can be found decorated with rime. When the coverage is especially heavy, so that the assembly looks like a tiny snowball, the result is called *graupel*.

The first two pictures at the right have relatively light rime coverage. The final example is completely covered with rime, but you can still see the six-fold symmetry of the underlying stellar crystal.

Irregular Crystals

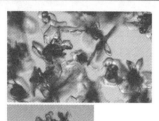

The most common snow crystals by far are the irregular crystals. These are small, usually clumped together, and show little of the symmetry seen in stellar or columnar crystals.

Artificial Snow

Snowmaking machines shoot a mixture of water and compressed air out of nozzles. The water comes out as fine droplets, and the air cools as it decompresses, causing the droplets to freeze. A fan blows the ice particles onto the slopes.

You can see from the picture at the right that artificial snow is made of frozen water droplets, with none of the elaborate structure found in real snow crystals.

Man-made snow may look like real snow, but look at the difference between it and the real thing. Because the ice crystals of man-made snow are not born in the very cold reaches of Earth's atmosphere, they do not get to form into beautiful flakes. It's great to ski on, but it's certainly not as pretty as the real thing!

Tracking a Snowstorm

One of the most frequent questions I am asked by students is, "How do you know when a snowstorm is coming?" Let's take a look at a storm as it develops and track it across the country.

Most big snowstorms need just two things to really make a lot of snow. They need lots of moisture and lots of cold, preferably arctic, air. It's common for a low to develop over the Central Plains and head southeastward. Let's position that low in Texas near Dallas on a Monday at 12 P.M. It is heading east, through the southeastern United States. High pressure—our preferred arctic air mass—is sitting over the Great Lakes and sinking south from Canada.

As the low moves eastward, a cold front trails south from it. Warm air is ahead of the front. As the low works eastward through the south, it produces soaking rains and thunderstorms while picking up tons of moisture from the Gulf of Mexico. When that moisture moves north and hits colder air, it produces snow through Tennessee, Kentucky, and the Ohio Valley.

By midnight Monday, the low is over Atlanta, and thunderstorms are dumping heavy rain over Georgia, South Carolina, and Florida. As the warm front pushes northward into the colder air, snow breaks out over the mid-Atlantic states, the Smokey Mountains, and the Virginias. By noon Tuesday, the low is over Washington, D.C., producing snow, and the arctic high is sliding eastward over New England.

Now the low is moving northeastward and out over the Atlantic Ocean, where conditions cause the low to strengthen. As the low becomes stronger it throws more moisture from the ocean back into the northeastern United States, creating a major snowstorm. In this scenario as much as 20 to 30 inches of snow can be produced throughout New England and the other northeastern states. By midnight

Tuesday, the storm is just east of Boston.

Types of Winter Precipitation

In winter, one of the hardest things for a weather forecaster to do is to figure out what type of precipitation there will be. In most cases winter storms bring more than just snow. Only in the coldest months in the northernmost reaches of the country is the precipitation usually all snow. Over much of the country, depending on local geography and the flow of just a little warm air, precipitation can vary from snow, sleet, or freezing rain (which causes many more automobile accidents than snow). Sometimes it is hard for forecasters to say exactly what is going to fall from the sky in winter because it's not just snow.

Other Kinds of Ice

There is always confusion when it comes to the names of the types of ice falling from the sky. Many people confuse sleet with hail. The difference is easy to remember: sleet in winter and hail in summer. But when it

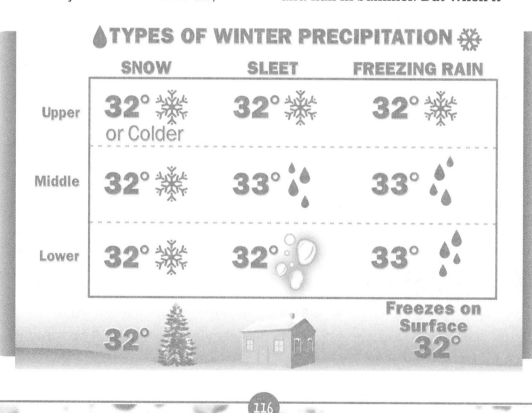

TYPES OF WINTER PRECIPITATION

	SNOW	SLEET	FREEZING RAIN
Upper	32° or Colder	32°	32°
Middle	32°	33°	33°
Lower	32°	32°	33°

32°

Freezes on Surface 32°

comes to ice and its classifications, not even scientists can agree.

Snow makes up seven of the ten kinds of frozen precipitation in the international classification system. The others are graupel, hail, and ice pellets or sleet. Official weather observers in the United States use the term *ice pellets* rather than sleet, as sleet is defined differently throughout the world. Here you can see the differences.

Wind Chill!

Whenever you hear the words "wind chill," it's because the cold winds are cranking outside. Wind chill is actually how skin feels when exposed to bitter winter winds. Updated in 2001 by the National Weather Service, the Wind Chill Temperature Index uses science, technology, and computer modeling to derive the Wind Chill Chart, which lets you know how it really feels outside.

The chart is based on the model of a human face, with wind blowing at an average height of 5 feet (the

Wind Chill Chart

Temperature (°F)																	
Calm	40	35	30	25	20	15	10	5	0	-5	-10	-15	-20	-25	-30	-35	-40	-45
5	36	31	25	19	13	7	1	-5	-11	-16	-22	-28	-34	-40	-46	-52	-57	-63
10	34	27	21	15	9	3	-4	-10	-16	-22	-28	-35	-41	-47	-53	-59	-66	-72
15	32	25	19	13	6	0	-7	-13	-19	-26	-32	-39	-45	-51	-58	-64	-71	-77
20	30	24	17	11	4	-2	-9	-15	-22	-29	-35	-42	-48	-55	-61	-68	-74	-81
25	29	23	16	9	3	-4	-11	-17	-24	-31	-37	-44	-51	-58	-64	-71	-78	-84
30	28	22	15	8	1	-5	-12	-19	-26	-33	-39	-46	-53	-60	-67	-73	-80	-87
35	28	21	14	7	0	-7	-14	-21	-27	-34	-41	-48	-55	-62	-69	-76	-82	-89
40	27	20	13	6	-1	-8	-15	-22	-29	-36	-43	-50	-57	-64	-71	-78	-84	-91
45	26	19	12	5	-2	-9	-16	-23	-30	-37	-44	-51	-58	-65	-72	-79	-86	-93
50	26	19	12	4	-3	-10	-17	-24	-31	-38	-45	-52	-60	-67	-74	-81	-88	-95
55	25	18	11	4	-3	-11	-18	-25	-32	-39	-46	-54	-61	-68	-75	-82	-89	-97
60	25	17	10	3	-4	-11	-19	-26	-33	-40	-48	-55	-62	-69	-76	-84	-91	-98

Wind (mph)

Frostbite Times ▮ 30 minutes ▯ 10 minutes ▯ 5 minutes

Wind Chill (°F) = 35.74 + 0.6215T - 35.75(V$^{0.16}$) + 0.4275T(V$^{0.16}$)

Where, T= Air Temperature (°F) V= Wind Speed (mph)

Effective 11/01/01

average height of an adult human face) and measures temperature against wind speed. Wind chill is computed using modern heat transfer theory (heat loss from the body to its surroundings during cold and breezy or windy days). Impact from the sun is not factored in as that may increase wind-chill temperatures by 10° to 18°F (-12° to -8°C). Wind chill can only be figured for temperatures at or below 50°F (10°C) and wind speeds above 3 mph.

Oh My, I Can't Feel My Fingers!

Coldest Temperatures Recorded in Each State

STATE	TEMPERATURE	LOCATION	DATE
Alabama	-27°F (-33°C)	New Market	January 30, 1966
Alaska	-80°F (-62°C)	Prospect Creek Camp	January 23, 1971
Arizona	-41°F (-41°C)	Hawley Lake	January 7, 1971
Arkansas	-29°F (-34°C)	Pond and Gavette	February 13, 1905
California	-45°F (-43°C)	Boca	January 20, 1937
Colorado	-61°F (-52°C)	Maybell	February 1, 1985
Connecticut	-37°F (-38°C)	Norfolk (Valley Station)	February 16, 1943
Delaware	-17°F (-27°C)	Millsboro	January 17, 1983
Florida	-2°F (-19°C)	Tallahassee	February 13, 1899
Georgia	-17°F (-27°C)	CCC camp F16 (Lafayette)	January 27, 1940
Hawaii	12°F (-11°C)	Mauna Kea Observatory Station	May 17, 1979
Idaho	-60°F (-51°C)	Island Park Dam	January 18, 1943
Illinois	-36 °F (-38°C)	Congerville	January 5, 1995
Indiana	-36 °F (-38°C)	New Whitehead	January 19, 1994
Iowa	-47°F (-44°C)	Elkader	February 3, 1996
Kansas	-40°F (-40°C)	Lebanon	February 13, 1905
Kentucky	-37°F (-38°C)	Shelbyville	January 19, 1994
Louisiana	-16°F (-27°C)	Minden	February 13, 1899
Maine	-48°F (-44°C)	Van Buren	January 19, 1925

STATE	TEMPERATURE	LOCATION	DATE
Maryland	-40°F (-40°C)	Oakland	January 13, 1912
Massachusetts	-40°F (-40°C)	Chester	January 12,1984
Michigan	-51°F (-46°C)	Vanderbilt	February 9, 1934
Minnesota	-60°F (-51°C)	Tower	February 2, 1996
Mississippi	-19°F (-28°C)	Corinth	January 30, 1996
Missouri	-40°F (-40°C)	Warsaw	February 13, 1905
Montana	-70°F (-57°C)	Rogers Pass	January 20, 1954
Nebraska	-47°F (-44°C)	Camp Clarke	February 12, 1899
Nevada	-50°F (-46°C)	San Jacinto	January 8, 1937
New Hampshire	-47°F (-44°C)	Mount Washington	January 31, 1934
New Jersey	-34°F (-36°C)	River Vale	January 5, 1904
New Mexico	-50°F (-46°C)	Gavilan	February 1, 1951
New York	-52°F (-47°C)	Old Forge	February 18, 1979
North Carolina	-34°F (-37°C)	Mount Mitchell	January 21, 1985
North Dakota	-60°F (-51°C)	Parshall	February 15, 1936
Ohio	-39°F (-39°C)	Milligan	February 10, 1899
Oklahoma	-27°F (-33°C)	Watts	January 18, 1930
Oregon	-54°F (-48°C)	Seneca	February 10, 1933
Pennsylvania	-42°F (-41°C)	Smethport	January 5, 1904
Rhode Island	-25°F (-32°C)	Greene	February 5, 1996
South Carolina	-22°F (-30°C)	Hogsback Mountain	January 21, 1985
South Dakota	-58°F (-50°C)	McIntosh	February 17, 1936
Tennessee	-32°F (-36°C)	Mountain City	December 30, 1917
Texas	-23°F (-31°C)	Seminole	February 8, 1933
Utah	-69°F (-56°C)	Peter's Sink	February 1, 1985
Vermont	-50°F (-46°C)	Bloomfield	December 30, 1933
Virginia	-30°F (-34°C)	Mountain Lake	January 22, 1985
Washington	-48°F (-44°C)	Mazama	December 30, 1968
West Virginia	-37°F (-38°C)	Lewisburg	December 30, 1917
Wisconsin	-55°F (-48°C)	Couderay	February 1, 1996
Wyoming	-63°F (-52°C)	Moran	February 1, 1933

You've Got to Be Kidding Me—Antarctica!

You want to talk about extremes, Antarctica is the land of extremes! It is the *coldest, windiest,* and *highest* continent anywhere on Earth! The lowest temperature ever recorded on the planet was -128.6°F (-89.2°C), was measured at the Russian research station of Vostok, near the South Pole, at an elevation of 11,220 feet. That's the same height as the Wasatch Mountains in Utah.

Antarctica has an average elevation of 7,544 feet (2,300 meters) above sea level. Even though it is covered in ice, it receives almost the least amount of rainfall of any place in the world, getting just slightly more rainfall than the Sahara Desert. Despite the snow and ice, Antarctica is the *largest desert* on Earth.

On July 4, 2003, a remote-recording weather station located on Queen Maud Land in eastern Antarctica reported an air temperature of -94°F (-70°C) and a wind speed of 75 mph. The resulting wind chill of -150°F (-101°C) is perhaps the coldest ever recorded anywhere. It's difficult to even imagine how a human could endure such extreme conditions!

How Low Can It Go?

Antarctica

Antarctica	-128.6°F (-89.2°C)	Vostok
	coldest official temperature in the world, on July 21, 1983	

The Arctic

Greenland	-86.8°F (-66°C)	Northice
North Pole	-59°F (-51°C)	North Pole

Asia

Russia	-90°F (-68°C)	Verkhoyansk
Mongolia	-72°F (-58°C)	Uvs Lake
Afghanistan	-64°F (-53°C)	Sharak
China	-62.1°F (-52.3°C)	Mohe
Turkey	-50°F (-46°C)	Karakose
Korea	-46°F (-43°C)	Chungangjin, N. Korea
Japan	-42°F (-41°C)	Asahikawa, Hokkaido
Iran	-33°F (-36°C)	Bijar and Saqquz
India	-24°F (-31°C)	Leh
Lebanon	-9°F (-23°C)	Yammoune
Pakistan	-8°F (-22°C)	Sakardu
Taiwan	-1°F (-18°C)	Yushan North Peak
Iraq	0°F (-18°C)	Mossul
Syria	4°F (-16°C)	Al Qamishi
Israel	6°F (-14°C)	Mount Avital
Jordan	7°F (-14°C)	Shoubak
Saudi Arabia	12°F (-11°C)	Turuyfa

Burma	21°F (-6°C)	Haka
Kuwait	21°F (-6°C)	Kuwait City
Sri Lanka	25°F (-4°C)	Nuwara Eliya
Laos	26°F (-3°C)	Xiang Khoang
Thailand	28°F (-2°C)	Doi Inthanon
Vietnam	28°F (-2°C)	Muong Bu
Hong Kong	32°F (0°C)	Victoria Peak
Oman	32°F (0°C)	Hibra
Yemen	32°F (0°C)	Sanaa
Bangladesh	33°F (1°C)	Jalpaiguri
Indonesia	34°F (1°C)	Mount Pangrango
Qatar	34°F (1°C)	Doha
Malaysia	36°F (2°C)	Cameron Highlands
Bahrain	37°F (3°C)	Manama
United Arab Emirates	37°F (3°C)	Sharjah
Philippines	37.5°F (3.1°C)	Baguio
Cambodia	46°F (8°C)	Val d'Emeraude
Maldives	64°F (18°C)	Male
Brunei	65°F (18°C)	Bandar Seri Bagawan
Singapore	65°F (18°C)	Paya Lebar

North America

Canada	-81.4°F (-63°C)	Snag, Yukon
United States	-79.8°F (-62°C)	Prospect Creek, AK
Mexico	-18.5°F (-28°C)	Los Lamentos
Cuba	32°F (0°C)	Havana Airport

Europe

| Russia | -68.8°F (-56°C) | Pechora |
| Sweden | -63°F (-53°C) | Vuoggatjalme |

Norway	-62°F (-52°C)	Karasjok
Finland	-61°F (-52°C)	Kittilä and Pokka
Armenia	-51°F (-41°C)	Paghakn
Estonia	-46°F (-43°C)	Jõgeva
Latvia	-46°F (-43°C)	Daugavpils
Yugoslavia (former)	-45°F (-43°C)	Igman, Bosnia Herzegovina
Czech Republic	-44°F (-42°C)	Litvínovice
Switzerland	-43.2°F (-41.7°C)	La Brevine
Poland	-42°F (-41°C)	Siedlce
Slovakia	-42°F (-41°C)	Viglas-Pstrusa
France	-41.5°F (-40.8°C)	Mouthe
Bulgaria	-38°F (-39°C)	Trun
Romania	-37°F (-38°C)	Bod
Iceland	-36.4°F (-38°C)	Grimsstadir and Modrudalur
Germany	-36°F (-37°C)	Hull
Italy	-36°F (-37°C)	Livigno
Austria	-35°F (-37°C)	Sonnblick
Hungary	-31°F (-35°C)	Gorombolytapolca
Spain	-28°F (-33°C)	Estany Gento
Denmark	-24.2°F (-31.2°C)	Horsted
Belgium	-22.2°F (-30.1°C)	Rochefort
Greece	-18°F (-28°C)	Ptolemaida
Great Britain	-17°F (-27°C)	Braemer and Altnaharra
Netherlands	-17°F (-27°C)	Winterswijk
Albania	-16°F (-27°C)	Sheqeras
Luxembourg	-12°F (-24°C)	Wiltz and Clemency
Ireland	-2°F (-19°C)	Markree Castle
Portugal	3°F (-16°C)	Penhas da Sude
Holy See	19°F (-7°C)	Vatican City
Cyprus	21°F (-6°C)	Nicosia
Azores	37°F (2.8°C)	Santa Cruz

South and Central America

Argentina	-38°F (-39°C)	Pato Superior Valley
Chile	-26°F (-32°C)	Ollague
Bolivia	-15°F (-26°C)	Uyuni
Peru	-13°F (-25°C)	Imata
Brazil	7°F (-14°C)	Cacador
Guatemala	12°F (-11°C)	Labor Ovalle
Uruguay	12°F (-11°C)	Melo
Costa Rica	16°F (-9°C)	Mount Chirripo
Ecuador	17°F (-8°C)	Romerillos
Paraguay	19°F (-7°C)	Prats Gill
Venezuela	19°F (-7°C)	El Aguila Peak
Colombia	20°F (-7°C)	Bogotá
Honduras	31°F (-0.5°C)	La Esperanza
Panama	36°F (2°C)	Bajo Grande
El Salvador	45°F (7°C)	San Salvadore
Belize	52°F (11°C)	Belize City
French Guiana	54°F (12°C)	Saul
Guyana	60°F (16°C)	Mazaruni
Suriname	60°F (16°C)	Paramaribo

Who Gets the Most Snow in the United States?

STATE	SNOWFALL IN INCHES	LOCATION
Alabama	5.3	Valley Head
Alaska	551.5	Thompson Pass
Arizona	243.0	Sunrise Mountain
Arkansas	16.2	Gravette
California	470.7	Soda Springs
Colorado	435.6	Wolf Creek Pass
Connecticut	106.8	Norfolk
Delaware	19.6	Wilmington

STATE	SNOWFALL IN INCHES	LOCATION
Florida	0.4	Milton Experiment Station
Georgia	6.6	Clayton
Hawaii	0	(Sorry!)
Idaho	283.5	Mullan Pass
Illinois	47.7	Antioch
Indiana	76.6	South Bend
Iowa	43.8	Dubuque
Kansas	46.0	McDonald
Kentucky	46.4	Benham
Louisiana	1.9	Plain Dealing
Maine	118.5	Phillips
Maryland	95.9	Oakland
Massachusetts	85.0	West Cummington
Michigan	235.8	Herman
Minnesota	108.5	Pigeon River Bridge
Mississippi	4.9	Cleveland
Missouri	25.5	Bethany
Montana	305.5	Kings Hill
Nebraska	62.2	Harrison
Nevada	241.0	Marlette Lake
New Hampshire	315.4	Mount Washington
New Jersey	39.8	Sussex
New Mexico	164.9	Red River
New York	226.7	Old Forge
North Carolina	57.8	Grandfather Mountain
North Dakota	56.5	Bowman
Ohio	97.0	Chardon
Oklahoma	31.6	Boise City
Oregon	529.9	Crater Lake

BLIZZARDS

STATE	SNOWFALL IN INCHES	LOCATION
Pennsylvania	121.6	Corry
Rhode Island	55.5	North Foster
South Carolina	8.7	Caesars Head
South Dakota	193.0	Lead
Tennessee	55.5	North Forester
Texas	23.9	Borger
Utah	516.3	Alta
Vermont	222.0	Mount Mansfield
Virginia	51.8	Burkes Garden
Washington	680.0	Rainier Paradise Ranger Station
West Virginia	157.8	Terra Alta
Wisconsin	138.7	Gurney
Wyoming	285.0	Belcher Ranger Station

HOW HIGH CAN IT CLIMB?—SNOWFALL RECORDS

SNOWFALL IN INCHES	LOCATION	POPULATION
203.4	Truckee, CA	13,800
179.8	Marquette, MI (airport)	
173.3	Steamboat Springs, CO	10,000
153.3	Oswego, NY	18,000
131.2	Sault Ste. Marie, MI	16,600
120.2	Syracuse, NY	147,300
118.2	Marquette, MI (city)	19,600
111.2	Meadville, PA	13,700
111.1	Flagstaff, AZ	53,000
110.8	Watertown, NY	26,700
105.9	Muskegon, MI	40,100
99.5	Rochester, NY	219,800
98.5	Utica, NY	60,600
97.9	Montpelier, NY	8,100
96.8	Traverse City, MI	14,500
95.7	Buffalo, NY	292,700
95.3	Juneau, AK	30,700
93.2	Presque Isle, ME	9,600
91.3	Cortland, NY	18,700
85.6	Casper, WY	49,700
83.3	Duluth, MN	87,700
82.6	Berlin, NH	10,300
81.6	Burlington, VT	38,900

TWENTY SNOWIEST LOCATIONS IN THE WILD WILD WEST

SNOWFALL IN INCHES	LOCATION
680	Paradise Ranger Station, Mount Rainier, WA
552	Thompson Pass, AK
530	Mount Baker Lodge, WA
530	Crater Lake, OR
516	Alta, UT
471	Soda Springs, CA
445	Tamarack, CA
442	Stampede Pass, WA
436	Wolf Creek Pass, CO
429	Silver Lake Brighton, UT
395	Twin Lakes, CA
328	Valdez, AK
300	Kings Hill, MT
285	Bechler River Ranger Station, WY
283	Mullan Pass, ID
276	Snake River, WY
271	Climax, CO
265	Silver Lake, CO
257	Government Camp, OR
254	Holden Village, WA

Snowiest Places in the Whole Wide World!

What comes to mind when you think about the snowiest places in the world? Do you think of Siberia, the Alps, or Mount Everest? Actually, North America is the snowiest continent on Earth. What location comes in second?

It's the Japanese Alps of Honshu Island, where scientists have measured the greatest snow depths on the planet. An incredible 466 inches (38.8 feet) was recorded at the 5,000-foot level of Mount Ibuki in 1927. The snowiest sea-level location in the world outside of Valdez, Alaska, can be found along Japan's coast. The town of Takada, which sits on the Sea of Japan, averages over 262 inches (21.8 feet) of snowfall in a season. In a single month, January 1945, the town recorded 362 inches (30.1 feet) of snow. In just 24 hours on February 8, 1927, 58.6 inches (4.9 feet) fell.

The Alps of France and Switzerland are probably the snowiest regions of the world, after North America and Japan. Snowfalls above the 6,000-feet level average 200 to 600 inches (50 feet) each winter. In the Swiss Alps, Santis, at 8,200 feet, gets an average of 570 inches (47.5 feet) each winter. Bessans, in the French Alps region of Savoie, once received 67.8 inches (5.7 feet) of snow in a 19-hour period. This is one of the most intense and extreme snowfalls on record anywhere in the world.

Italy is also known for extreme snowfalls. The town of Montevegrine, in the southern Apennines, once had 54.4 inches (4.5 feet) of snow fall in 24 hours. In Sicily, the town of Floresta recorded 51.2 inches (42.7 feet) in 24 hours on February 22, 1929.

When one thinks of snow, Russia always comes to mind. Every part of that country experiences some kind of snow in winter. Many people think that Siberia has huge snowfalls, but it doesn't. Siberia is so cold and dry that often it gets no more than 20 to 30 inches (1.7 to 2.5 feet) of snow in a year. In contrast, the Western Great Caucasus near Turkey and the Black Sea can have accumulations of 150 to 200 inches

(12.5 to 16.7 feet) in one winter. Talk about extreme!

Great Britain's greatest storm took place in only 15 hours. A near world record snow of 70.9 inches (5.9 feet) fell on Dartmoor on February 16, 1929. Norway, too, is a big snow producer—the Jostedalsbreen Mountains at Fanaraken rake in more than 400 inches (33 feet) of snow in a season. Also in Scandinavia, Sweden's Kebnekaise Mountains see accumulations of 240 inches (16.7 feet) of snow during the winters.

Holy Geez! I Didn't Know You Could Do That with Snow!

People can do some really cool stuff with snow.

I always love to make snowmen. One of my favorite cartoons is Calvin and Hobbs. Now this is my kind of "How to make a go in the snow!"

Homework, Schmomework! Calvin is da' man!

Nothing Like an Avalanche to Perk Up Your Day!

Technically, an avalanche is any amount of snow sliding down a mountainside. An avalanche can be compared to a landslide, only with snow instead of earth. People who live in areas that get a lot of snow also call avalanches "snowslides."

As an avalanche moves toward the bottom of a slope, it gains speed and power; this can cause even the smallest of avalanches to be a major disaster!

Many kinds of snow can form avalanches—it all depends on the region, temperature, and weather. Whether the snow is light and fluffy, wet, thick slabs, or flying powder, all avalanches are potentially very dangerous.

Avalanches happen on mountains where extreme amounts of snow fall and build up. They claim about 150 lives a year worldwide, with hundreds more injured or trapped. Don't ski or hike in areas that are marked off due to a possible avalanche!

Need to Control an Avalanche? Let's Blow It Up!

Only experts are allowed to "create" an avalanche. By deliberately triggering a small, hopefully controlled avalanche, mountain experts hope to release the stresses on the snow that might cause a large, uncontrolled avalanche.

Percussion guns, explosives, and even artillery have been used to produce these controlled avalanches. When an avalanche is to be set off, warnings are issued and people are kept away from areas of potential danger.

Release the Hounds!

Avalanche dogs are a must on any mountain, large or small, and even in flat regions where snow sports are popular. Skiing, hiking, snowboarding, and just about any other snow-related activity you can imagine create plenty of opportunities for accidents. Children get lost, elderly people fall and get covered by snow, and, of course, avalanches are all great reasons to have an avalanche dog around.

In the 1930s, the Swiss Army came up with the idea of using a dog's superior sense of smell to locate people buried in the snow. Once a person is buried in the snow, detection is impossible with the naked eye, but rescue dogs can pick up the human scent easily, making a live recovery possible.

Training is intense. It often takes three years of dedication for the dog as well as the handler before the team is proficient at finding victims in the snow. The dog is taught to not only locate humans, but to also alert everyone and to dig out the victim!

Now that's a gooooooooood doggie!

Let's Melt It, Dude!

Rather than hauling the snow away and dumping it in rivers, many cities are now using huge snowmelters. It can melt fourteen dump-truck loads in an hour!

I Didn't Know It Could Snow That Hard!

SNOWFALL IN INCHES	TIME	LOCATION	DATE
5.0	20 minutes	Turin, NY	December 22, 1993
6.0	30 minutes	Copenhagen, NY	December 2, 1966
12.0	1 hour	Copenhagen, NY	December 2, 1966
17.5	2 hours	Oswego, NY	January 26, 1972
27.0	3.5 hours	Oswego, NY	January 26, 1972
36.0	9 hours	Adams, NY	January 18, 1993
40.0	12 hours	Montague Township, NY	January 11–12, 1997
70.9*	15 hours	Dartmoor, Great Britain	February 16, 1929
51.0	16 hours	Bennett Ridge, NY	January 17–18, 1959
67.8	19 hours	Bessans, France	April 5–6, 1959
62.0	22 hours	Freye's Ranch, CO	April 14–15, 1952
54.4	24 hours	Montevergine, Italy	February 22, 1929
55.0	24 hours	Alta, UT	January 5–6, 1994
56.0	24 hours	Randolf, NH	November 23–24, 1943
57.1	24 hours	Tahtsa Lake, BC, Canada	February 11, 1999
58.6	24 hours	Takada, Honshu, Japan	February 8, 1927
63.0	24 hours	Georgetown, CO	December 4, 1913
65.0	24 hours	Crystal Mountain, WA	January 23–24, 1943
67.0	24 hours	Echo Summit, CA	January 4, 1982
68.0	24 hours	Squaw Valley, CA	January 1, 1997
68.2	24 hours	Tsukayama, Japan	December 30–31, 1960
75.8	24 hours	Silver Lake, CO	April 14–15, 1927

SNOWFALL IN INCHES	TIME	LOCATION	DATE
77.0*	24 hours	Montague Township, NY	January 11–12, 1997
84.0*	24 hours	Crestview C.H. Dept, CA	January 14–15, 1952
87.0	27.5 hours	Silver Lake, CO	April 14–15, 1927
95.0	32.5 hours	Silver Lake, CO	April 14–15, 1927
120.6	2 days	Thompson Pass, AK	December 29–30, 1955
129.0	3 days	Laconia, WA	February 24–26, 1910
147.0	3 days	Thompson Pass, AK	December 28–30, 1955
194.0*	4 days	Norden, CA	April 20–23, 1880
189.0	6 days	Mount Shasta, CA	February 13–19, 1959
424.0	30 days	Tamarack, CA	January–February 1911
362.2	1 month	Takada, Japan	January 1945
363.0	1 month	Paradise Ranger Station, WA	January 1925
390.0	1 month	Tamarack, CA	January 1911
503.0	2 months	Summit, CA	December 1894–January 1895
504.0	2 months	Paradise Ranger Station, WA	January–February 1945
710.5	3 months	Mount Baker, WA	December 1998–February 1999
1107.0	6 months	Mount Baker, WA	October 1998–April 1999
963.2	12 months	Revelstoke Mt., BC, Canada	1971–1972
974.4	12 months	Thompson Pass, AK	1952–1953
1122.0	12 months	Paradise Ranger Station, WA	1971–1972
1140.0	12 months	Mount Baker, WA	1998–1999

* unofficial measurements

A New York Story: The Coldest Day Ever in New York City!

New York City has a great history when it comes to snow and cold, captured not only in pictures, but also in the stories that accompany some of the greatest weather moments in the history of the Big Apple. Cold waves and blizzards are the highlights of over three centuries of record keeping in New York City.

A massive cold wave swept the Northeast in 1857. January of that year is the coldest month ever recorded in New England. The average temperatures of 16.7°F (-8.5°C) in New Haven, 16.8°F (-8.4°C) in Boston, and 19.6°F (-6.9°C) in New York City remain the coldest months on record. On the 23rd of that month, the Smithsonian thermometer at Erasmus Hall in Brooklyn, New York, reached a high temperature of 0°F

PUBLISHED BY CURRIER & IVES   THE CURRIER & IVES FOUNDATION

CENTRAL PARK IN WINTER.

PUBISHED IN 1862 BY CURRIER & IVES

THE CURRIER & IVES FOUNDATION

CENTRAL-PARK, WINTER:
THE SKATING POND

(-17.8°C). The Hudson River froze over solidly enough that small food and shop carts could be set up on the river. It was solid enough for people to walk back and forth to New Jersey. That cold wave was captured by Currier and Ives in their two famous prints of New York City and Central Park.

There are several famous blizzards in New York City's history, but none so extreme or bizarre as the Blizzard of 1888. March is a month of extremes as far as temperatures go, and March 1888 was truly extreme. Friday, March 9, 1888, had been the warmest day of the year; shopkeepers advertised SPRING OPENING DAY, and city residents enjoyed balmy weekend temperatures in the 50s! Walt Whitman wrote a poem for the *New York Herald* that ended with the line, "The spring's first dandelion shows its true face."

But on the morning of Monday, March 12, commuters were caught off guard. A heavy whiteout type of snow fell all day long. Wind gusts were above hurricane strength at 80 mph. Snowdrifts piled above 20 feet. By afternoon, the city was

Digging out in Flushing, New York, after the Blizzard of 1888.

A train wreck caused by the Blizzard of 1888.

smothered in a blanket of white. Power and telephone lines had fallen throughout the boroughs. Thousands of commuters were trapped in unheated elevated trains, and horse-drawn carriages were stuck in the drift-filled streets.

The New York Stock Exchange closed for the first time due to weather since it had opened in 1792. The ferries stopped running and Broadway theaters closed. More than two hundred ships were wrecked off New York Harbor that day.

The blizzard caused at least two hundred deaths in New York City. After the storm, frozen bodies were recovered from snowdrifts. Livery drivers froze to death in the cabs of their carriages. Horses died in harness. Two hundred more people died throughout the Northeast.

All this devastation did have a silver lining. The events of the blizzard led the city to begin burying telephone and electrical wiring, and to build an underground subway system that is currently the largest in the world.

However, true to the New York way of life, during that infamous blizzard, Daly's Theatre did not disappoint the few, intrepid theatergoers who battled 20-foot snowdrifts to get to that evening's performance of Shakespeare. What

show was it? You guessed it! *A Midsummer Night's Dream*! As they say on Broadway, "The show must go on!"

The Storm of the Century

On March 7, 1993, I was working in the weather office at WABC-TV in New York City, getting ready for another day of TV and radio broadcasts, when I noticed what appeared to be a potentially significant storm developing over the American Southwest.

Experience told me that this storm would likely blow through the Southeast and then turn up the East Coast—and that it would be messy. Boy, was it ever! This storm came to define extreme for a blizzard. Snowfall amounts averaged 2 feet— an average of 24 inches of snow fell onto most places from the

MECHANICS BEHIND THE MARCH BLIZZARD OF 1993

POLAR JET

PACIFIC JET

SUBTROPICAL JET

ALL MERGED INTO ONE

2004 WWW.ACCUWEATHER.COM

southeastern United States, up the Eastern Seaboard to New England. From Maine to Georgia, snow and high winds buried the East Coast. Snow fell on nearly every inch of Alabama, a very rare occurrence. Seventeen inches alone fell in Birmingham, Alabama. This event, which lasted from March 12th to the 15th in the United States, came to be known as the Storm of the Century!

The storm was of biblical proportions. We had a reporter doing a live shot at a Long Island beach. As tropical storm–force winds of 55 mph blasted his face with snow, ice, and flying sand, he proclaimed, "All we need now is a plague of locusts!" Eighteen homes on Long Island were washed into the sea due to the pounding surf and many marinas were damaged or destroyed.

Half the states in the United States were affected in one way or another. In Florida, a 12-foot storm surge killed seven people, and a nasty outbreak of fifty tornadoes

took eighteen lives. Three million people lost power, 270 people died on land, and 48 more were lost at sea. Powerful waves hammered the Northeast coast.

As you can see, a blizzard can bring plenty of destruction as well as a lot of snow! The estimated cost of the cleanup was $6 billion.

Record amounts of snow fell on places that normally do not get a lot of snow. The Florida Panhandle received half a foot of snow. Chattanooga, Tennessee, which normally sees about 4 inches of snow in a season, got blanketed with 20 inches. The New York City area averaged 24 to 29 inches of snow. Powerful, howling winds blew out windows from skyscrapers, raining glass daggers onto those below.

Syracuse, New York, was pounded with 43 inches of snow. In Georgia, 1.3 million chickens died. Atlanta issued its first blizzard warning in history as the city received 9 inches of snow. Two hundred hikers had to be rescued by helicopter in the Great Smokey Mountains, where 4 feet of snow fell. Boston cancelled its St. Patrick's Day Parade for the first time ever. Winds were recorded in the Florida Keys at 109 mph . . . and the storm was just beginning! The winds at Mount Washington, New Hampshire, raced across the

Presidential Range, gusting to 144 mph. The temperature in Burlington, Vermont, plunged to -12° F (-24.4°C). The record low pressure of the storm, 28.38 inches at White Plains, New York, was blamed for an unusually high number of childbirths!

The total amount of snow was huge! The normal ratio of rain to snow is that 1 inch of liquid makes 10 inches of snow. If the air mass is colder, then even more snow can result. After the Storm of the Century, the National Weather Service reported that if the amount

of snow that fell had been rain, it would have been forty times the volume of water that flows out of the Mississippi River at New Orleans in one day! In another highlight, Mount Leconte in Tennessee received a whopping 56 inches of snow!

Can Somebody Toss Me a Shovel? I Gotta Get Outta Here!

I remember the storm vividly. New York City was smothered with 2 feet of snow. New Jersey had nearly 30 inches in Newark and Patterson. The snow piled high enough to cover the roofs of the cars that were unfortunately parked at curbside—cars that were buried even deeper when the snowplows came through. Many vehicles were left in place until the snow melted. I did a weather report standing on the top of a completely covered SUV. I dug out the top to show that the SUV was actually under there!

The Blizzard of 1996

Just three years later, another gigantic blizzard struck the East Coast. This was the second storm to have a huge impact on me, personally and professionally. I'll tell you about the first a little later.

It was Tuesday, January 2, 1996, and I was doing the weather live at 5 A.M. in beautiful Prospect Park, Brooklyn. I was riding a 60-inch Flexible Flyer sled (the greatest sled ever built!) that had been lent to me by a good friend and colleague, Fred Chieco. Flying down the snow-covered hills of that beautiful place in the morning sun on live television was a delight—until I had to tell New Yorkers of an impending blizzard that was soon to blast not only New York City, but the entire tristate area, New England, and the whole East Coast!

The only problem with the forecast was that the storm wouldn't reach the area until Sunday. I admit, predicting a blizzard five days before it was due to hit was risky. But the computer models had been very good at forecasting winter storms that year and I felt confident in their information, so I went with my gut and went public with my prediction. Everyone thought I was crazy!

Snow started falling Saturday afternoon, January 6, and by the time it stopped snowing early on Monday, January 8, the storm was as devastating as the blizzard of 1993. The snow was heaviest in the Virginias, Washington, D.C., Maryland, New Jersey, Connecticut, Ohio, Pennsylvania, New York, Massachusetts, and throughout New England. Most of the snowfall records from the Storm of the Century were broken.

The cost in damage, lost sales, and decreased production was estimated at nearly $17 billion. The New York City school system was closed for snow on that Monday, January 8, for the first time in 20 years. Then mayor Rudy Giuliani declared that no cars could come into the city. You could leave with your car, but you could not come back. Snow packed the streets so tightly even buses and garbage trucks could not pass.

In the Bronx, two armed gunmen robbed a building superintendent. The thieves weren't after his money; they took his snowblower!

Thousands of flights were canceled and travelers slept in airports up and down the entire East Coast. Travelers on United flight 801, which was supposed to fly from Kennedy Airport to Tokyo, were stranded in the plane on the runway for 7½ hours. One passenger reported later that the captain threatened to arrest people because they were getting too riotous.

Two feet of snow covered Dulles International Airport in Washington, D.C., which, in the two days of the storm, received more snow than what usually falls there in a whole year. All the highways in Illinois were shut down. A Metro train in the suburbs of Washington, D.C., slid and crashed into another train; one driver died.

In Frederick County, Maryland, the weight of the heavy snow collapsed a barn and killed one hundred cows.

Boston received 18 inches of snow, bringing the city's seasonal total to a record 32 inches. Philadelphia came to a standstill with 30 inches. The mail couldn't be delivered there.

In Pennsylvania, twenty-nine people died of heart attacks on January 8 as a result of shoveling driveways. Snow shoveling was dangerous in other ways: a 60-year-old man in an Allentown suburb accused his 70-year-old neighbor of shoveling snow onto his car; the angry neighbor pushed him down, and he died. Overall, ninety-nine Pennsylvanians died. Eighty of the deaths were due to the blizzard, the rest were from subsequent flooding.

The blizzard was not bad news for everyone. In Pocahontas County, West Virginia, a ski resort marveled at the 4 feet of snow that had accumulated.

As for me . . . despite my own forecast, on Saturday, January 6, three friends and I decided we could drive from New York City to Pittsburgh, catch the Pittsburgh Steelers and Buffalo Bills in an AFC playoff game, and get back to New

York before the storm was in full force. But my timing was a bit off. It began snowing in Pittsburgh, Philadelphia, and New York City about 6 hours ahead of schedule. We left Pittsburgh at 7 A.M. Sunday morning and began our drive—or plow, I should say—back to the city. Cars were pulling off to the sides of the highways, with passengers inside, and snow was beginning to cover them. I did phone-in reports live on WABC-TV from the SUV as we slowly trekked across Pennsylvania.

What should have been a 5-to-6-hour drive became a 17-hour drive! We constantly had to stop along the Pennsylvania Turnpike to clean our wiper blades and headlights. When we were halfway across the state, the Pennsylvania Turnpike Authority closed the highway! But we couldn't just stop on the highway and wait out the storm—we might have died. So we pressed on, traveling the closed turnpike, which wasn't going to be plowed anytime soon.

I had to get back. I had to be on the air! This is what a meteorologist lives for, to be on-camera during the "big one." I was on-air for what was thought to be the "big one" in 1993, and here it was happening all over again! I was supposed to be on camera at 4 A.M. Monday morning.

The storm would still be going, and I was determined to get to the studio.

We drove through toll plazas that looked like ghost towns. The turnpike was abandoned except for the occasional car trapped on the roadside. Soon, the snow piled so high on the roadway it was above the headlights of our SUV. We were plowing through it like a snowplow. It was amazing. However, I do not suggest or recommend that you or anyone do that!

We slowly worked our way across the Delaware River Bridge to the New Jersey Turnpike, the "thunder road." We heard on the radio that the state of New Jersey had officially closed the turnpike. Motorists were told to stay away as the road would not be plowed until the storm was nearly over. The snow was easily waist- to chest-deep on the turnpike. We drove on despite the blinding snow and howling winds—a total whiteout. I'm sure we wove over every lane of the four-lane turnpike. Our tire tracks were immediately wiped out by snow that seemed to be like sugar pouring from a container.

We made our way about halfway across New Jersey to Montclair. Exhausted, we decided to stop at a train station there, where I would try to make my way to New York City, and my friends would seek shelter at a neighboring home. We had heard on the radio that the trains were running on a very limited schedule. Trains with plows attached to the engine were clearing the tracks.

At 2 A.M., a train reached the station in Montclair. Great! I could make the broadcast at 4 A.M. The train pulled into Penn Station at 3 A.M. It looked as if the whole city of New York was in the train station, seeking refuge from the monster raging outside. When I got to the street, the wind was blasting at 50 mph. Snow was not only blowing sideways, the drifts reached up four stories on buildings!

Bags in hand, I ran up Eighth Avenue. The snow on the sidewalks was up to my waist, and even up to my chest in places where it had collected between the buildings. Who needs Mount Everest to climb?

I could tell it was going to take hours at this pace to make it to the television studios of WABC-TV. I needed a ride. But there were no cars, not even a police car. The city that never sleeps was desolate. It was now 3:30 A.M. and I was due on-air in 30 minutes. I was at Eighth Avenue and 47th Street—twenty blocks from the studio, which in N.Y.C. distance is one mile. In usual conditions, it would be no more than a 20-minute walk to the studio. But I could never trudge there in waist-deep snow before four o'clock.

But wait! Coming up Eighth, I saw headlights. It was a taxi! With its VACANT light on! What was he doing out in this weather? No one was out. The streets were a disaster. But I saw it as the cavalry arriving to save the day! I headed toward the taxi and I noticed it was stuck, spinning like crazy in a snow pack. I ran over and helped the driver by pushing the car and getting it going up the street again. I asked the driver if he would give me a ride to work. He agreed, and I got in. The driver said his name was Papa. He was from Senegal and had never seen snow before!

As we made our way up Eighth, I had to get out twice to push, but we made it to the studio at 3:50 A.M. A whole ten minutes to spare! I asked Papa what the fare was. He didn't know. He'd forgotten to start the meter! It wouldn't have mattered what the fare was, I was going to reward him handsomely for the rescue. I gave Papa a very large cash reward for his kindness to a stranger. Papa said I was his last fare and he was headed home. I hope he made it!

As I was getting ready to go on camera, the executive producer said to me, "That's a heck of a blizzard out there." I said, "You're right. You'd have to be a fool to go out in a storm like that."

Famous Snows

Ninety-six moviegoers died in the Knickerbocker Theatre in Washington, D.C., when heavy snows caved in the building's roof on January 29, 1922.

A snowstorm brought about the first case of cannibalism tried in the United States. In January 1874, Alfred Packer (sometimes spelled Alferd) led a team of prospectors into the San Juan Mountains of Colorado. At a camp near Montrose, the group of twenty-one men was advised not to cross the mountains because of snow. Packer and five others went anyway, and sometime in February or March, they got lost and snowbound. In April, Packer showed up at the Los Pinos Indian Agency alone. His companions were never seen. Human remains were found in August on the trail. Packer was eventually tried for cannibalism and sentenced to be hanged, but later his sentence was reduced to prison time. Some say that after the trial, he became a vegetarian. His legacy? He's a Colorado folk hero, and a cafeteria at the Boulder University Memorial Center is named the Alferd Packer Memorial Grill.

Animals in the Snow

On March 8, 1717, approximately 1,200 sheep that had been trapped in a snowstorm were found on Shelter Island in New York. They had been there for four weeks and only a hundred were still alive.

Four out of every five head of cattle in Kansas died in a raging blizzard on January 13, 1886.

A three-day blizzard that started on January 28, 1887, wiped out millions of free-range cattle in Montana. Cowboy "Teddy Blue" reported that by the time the "Big Die-Up" was over, more than 60 percent of Montana's cattle were dead. This snowy, cold winter hastened the end of the Old West's open range system, as people moved toward homesteading and ranching.

One million Thanksgiving turkeys froze to death in a South Dakota blizzard on November 18, 1943.

Over a foot of snow fell in Arkansas on January 6, 1988, killing 3.5 million chickens. Another 1,750,000 chickens died across the border in Texas. The following day, two million more chickens died in Alabama.

A Trip to -70 Below!

Cold, that's what! One of the coolest places on Earth for weather is in New Hampshire, atop Mount Washington. Before the Europeans arrived, Native Americans called it *Agiocochook*, "Home of the Great Spirit." During a wild storm in 1934, a gust of wind at 231 mph pushed across the summit. That wind speed still stands as the all-time surface-wind-speed record on Earth! Because of the mountain's unique location, with arctic air pouring in from Canada and its proximity to the Atlantic Ocean and the jet stream, it's a perfect spot for extreme weather.

Take for instance the recipe that created the record winds. A storm over the Great Lakes, a batch of energy off the coast of North Carolina, and a ridge of high pressure over Canada. It's a concoction that can only come together at this one place in the world. You have to take a trip there to the observatory. I did, and it turned into the story of a lifetime.

I took a producer and a cameraman to the observatory to do a feature story on the work the scientists do there. The first to climb Mount Washington was a guy named Darby Field back in 1642. In 1853—before the Civil War—Tip Top House was built and still stands today. Pretty good construction back then!

The observatory has been recording and disseminating weather information for more than one hundred years, since 1870. It also serves as a benchmark station, which means it's a climatic station with a long record of data obtained in a single location with no change in the environment of the station. It's a part of the Historical Climatic Network of the United States and is used for the measuring of cosmic ray activity in the upper atmosphere, developing robust instrumentation for severe weather environments, and conducting many types of severe weather research and testing. It is truly an interesting and provocative place.

On a summer day, if there's no traffic, you can drive to the top of Mount Washington in about five minutes. Everywhere in the Northeast you see vehicles with bumper stickers that say, "This vehicle climbed Mount Washington." I used to think how cool that must have been. In the 1970s, road rallies were held where race cars drove to the top in close to a minute.

But in winter, it's totally impossible to drive to the mountain's top in a car, a truck, or even an SUV. You can only get there by snowcat. So now, when I see those bumper stickers, I know that they made the trip in the summertime, and I always say to myself, "Hey, why don't you try it in winter?" Mount Washington is one of the coolest places and most bizarre places I have ever visited.

On our trip to the summit and the observatory, there had been plenty of snow and plenty of cold. At the bottom of the mountain, the sun was out and the wind was calm. It was postcard beautiful. The snowcat driver, a guy who could easily have passed for a *Top Gun* fighter pilot, calmly said, "Put on all your gear because it's a bear at the top." I thought to myself, "I lived through the Storm of the Century and the Blizzard of 1996; how much worse could it be?" We looked toward the top of the mountain but we could not see it because it was covered in clouds.

We took the snowcat to the top. The vehicle is heated, smooth-riding, and comfy. The ride lasted about 45 minutes to an hour. When we got to the top of the mountain and left the nice, toasty, comfy snowcat, it was as if we had been transported to the North Pole! The wind nearly knocked me to the ground. I grabbed the side of the snowcat and hung on. "Howling" does not even come close to describing the wind at that moment on Mount Washington. Words like "sledgehammer" come to mind. It's a very heavy, constant, lead-weight type of wind . . . except the lead was coming at us at 55 to 65 mph, and no human can stand upright in a wind of that speed.

The snowcat driver looked out his window at me and said, "That's nothing, weatherman; you are in for the experience of your life." He was right.

When I looked out across the summit, I thought I was on the moon. It was a crusty landscape of snow and ice. The mountain's slopes have rocky holes and jagged craters that resemble the surface of the moon. Locals call autumn "ankle-breaking season," because of the number of hikers injured by getting their ankles twisted in those jagged crevices.

We had dressed as though we were going to Antarctica. I had on two sets of thermal underwear, two pairs of thermal socks, insulated snow pants, a fleece top under a thermal jacket, and a heavy polar coat on top of that. I wore earmuffs, a thermal cap, and a knit cap over that. A face gaiter covered my entire face (it looked like a hockey mask), and ski goggles protected my eyes. I wore special insulated boots with crampons (ice spikes) attached. I also had a pair of ice climbers, very high-tech ice axes. I looked like a combination of the Michelin Man and Jason from *Friday the 13th*!

On our first day, the mountain scenery brought excitement, a bit of anxiousness, and a sizeable amount of fear. The wind had picked up to 55 to 60 mph; it would have been hard to stand up on dry ground, let alone on feet of ice. The crampons on our boots were the only thing that kept us from being blown away. Although we looked like Neil Armstrong bouncing around on the moon, we were able to work our

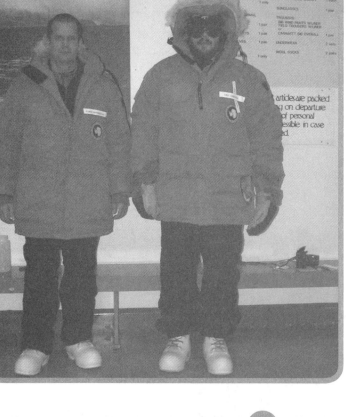

way around the observatory and admire the beauty of the rime ice that had collected on everything. The temperature was near 0°F (-17.8°C) and the windchill was -33°F (-36.1°C). We could stay out only 15 to 20 minutes in that cold at the very most, even with all our gear on.

We had to make it one of the fastest shoots I've ever done. We couldn't shoot longer than 15 minutes because the camera's lens and internal parts would freeze! Our personal still cameras and cell phones would not work for more than just a few minutes in the cold either. Once we earned the world record for shooting a story, we returned to the warmth of the observatory, which is a half-circular concrete and steel bunker. The structure is plenty strong, though it does make some eerie, creaky noises when the wind really gets going.

Mount Washington, by global standards, is a small peak; regardless, its weather can rival that of some of the most extreme and rugged places on earth. There are colder places, like Antarctica, and snowier places, like Alaska or the Cascade Range, but on this mountain, there are days each winter when the combination of life-threatening weather factors is similar to the extreme weather that

has been recorded in the polar regions and on peaks four times Mount Washington's height. We found this out firsthand.

After we awoke the next morning in the observatory, and as we packed our bags to head back down the mountain in the snowcat, the observatory staff gave us an update on the weather that was quite shocking. One of the biggest storms of the season was blowing in fast from Canada. The storm was forecast to be so cold and windy, we would not be able to get down from the mountain that day. The oil inside the snowcat would freeze in the extreme cold that was on the way! So we were stranded on top of Mount Washington for who knew how long.

The monster storm was due to arrive that evening after dark. We could tell that the wind was beginning to pick up by the sounds the observatory structure was making—moaning, creaking, and groaning—as the blasts of wind struck it. I wanted to feel the full force of this storm at its height.

The phones began ringing in the observatory. It was the staff back at the television station, wanting to know if we were okay. Radio stations and newspapers were also calling, to get interviews and updates on the storm, plus to find out how a meteorologist could get stuck in a snowstorm! We called our families to let them know that the mountain did not want us to leave.

As night came to Mount Washington, so did the abominable wind monster. I suited up with the crew to head outside to the observation platform, which was in the direct path of the wind. It was dark, but the lights of the observatory helped us to see the snow being blasted toward us. As I opened the door, the wind snapped my head back, causing the back of my head to hit the iron door. Ouch! Blurry-eyed, I crawled up the ladder with the wind and snow smashing me against the observatory. Had the structure not been behind me, I would have been blown away. You

can only hold on to the railing for so long before exhaustion sets in. I crouched down on the top of the platform, clinging to the rails for dear life. The noise was unbelievable. The wind *hurt*. Under all that protection, even my hair hurt!

I was terrified. I thought about what it must have been like for the people who have tried to brave this type of weather to climb this mountain. There have been 135 fatalities on Mount Washington since 1849, many of them involving ill-prepared hikers, skiers, and climbers. Many of them had no idea what they were facing. Many expected conditions at the top to be similar to those in the valley, only to find themselves, like me, in a whole different treacherous world.

The winds were clocked by the anemometer at 100 mph and the temperature was −20°F (-6.7°C). That gave us a wind chill of -69°F (-56.1°C)! What's that like? When I spit, it froze instantly in the air and hit the observatory as a piece of ice. I could see my breath as it came out. It

**Mount Washington,
New Hampshire**

made a hissing, crackling sound as it immediately froze. I found a square piece of thin ice and when I broke it, it sounded as if I had broken a piece of glass. The rime ice that coated the buildings—shaped by the high winds—made that same glass-shattering sound when we broke that, too. Where the ice was thick, I tried to hammer it with the ice ax, but the tool could not penetrate the ice and just bounced off. Once we got back to the iron door of the observatory, I took a cup of water and tossed it outside; it froze in the air instantly and blew past the building. Then I took a cup of hot coffee and tossed it outside; it, too, froze in the air and blew away. The sound of the water freezing was like crackling, and the hot coffee was even louder!

When I returned to the observatory and took off my gear, my face hurt. My nose burned, my feet and hands were frozen, and I was exhausted. Even through all that gear, the cold wind sent piercing daggers all though my aching body. I have stood outdoors in snowstorms, blizzards, and even hurricanes, but I have never experienced anything that compares to this.

The cold wind made its way through my face gaiter and burned the skin off my nose and forehead. I lost a couple of toenails and several of my fingernails turned black. To this day, when I go out in the cold, my fingers and toes remind me of that unforgettable adventure. I had heard that once you get frostbite, you are more likely to feel those effects again more quickly the next time you are in the cold, and now I know that's true.

Late the next day, we were able to leave the mountain. The storm had passed and the temperatures had warmed to levels at which the snowcat could operate. I couldn't believe the change in the conditions. It was sunny, with blue skies and no wind. It was absolutely serene and beautiful. The Presidential Range and Tuckerman's Ravine were covered in crystals and shining brilliantly. That's what you can run into at Mount Washington. One day horrific and the next day calm. We thanked the staff of Mount Washington Observatory for their hospitality and for keeping us safe, as well as for the learning experience. I would go back again in an instant—in the summertime!

Colored Snow

I'm sure you've heard the universal warnings, "Be careful, do not eat the yellow snow!" Yuk!

But, what if it tasted like watermelon? Yum, yum! Now that's extreme! In some mountainous areas, Colorado especially, it is not uncommon to find pink snow falling from the sky. The pink is caused by a type of alga called *Chlamydomonas nivalis*. It's called "watermelon snow" because it actually has a taste very similar to watermelon.

Can you image, walking outside after a snowfall and finding pink snow all over the ground? And it's safe to eat? At least the locals there say it is safe to eat . . . better in small quantities, I'm sure!

There are more than 350 kinds of algae that survive in very cold temperatures. These algae can turn the snow many colors, such as black, brown, or yellow. (Just don't confuse it with the other kind of yellow snow!)

Chlamydomonas nivalis tends to flourish when the weather warms a bit after the coldest of the winter. It starts out green, then turns pinkish or reddish as the sky brightens. The cells have a gelatinous sheath that protects them from the strong sunlight at high altitudes, and it is that sheath that produces the pink color.

Snow can be colored by other things like sand or soils that can make it appear brownish. Sandstorms in the Sahara lift soil into the air; atmospheric winds carry those particles long distances, such as over southern Europe, where the soil is combined with snow to produce brown or reddish snow.

Snow can be colored by soot from burning coal or wood. Volcanoes and Mongolian sandstorms also can make colored snow. Be careful in urban areas, where auto emissions and other toxins can be mixed in; eating that kind of snow might make you sick. Studies in 2008 from Louisiana State University have shown that different types of bacteria can gather on ice crystals in snow, and that eating it could be harmful.

On January 31, 2007, a weird colored snow fell over Russia. Oily yellow and orange snowflakes fell over 570 square miles (1,500 sq km) in the Omsk region. Russian officials said that they could not explain the snow, which was oily to the touch and had a pronounced rotten smell. Although the official cause is still a mystery, the snow contained four times the normal level of iron. The Russians believe it was the result of a chemical accident or from a rare dust hurricane in neighboring Kazakhstan! Wow! That's extreme!

Snow Rollers

I love the cartoons where a snowball starts at the top of the mountain and rolls all the way down the mountainside, growing bigger and bigger, moving faster and faster, collecting anything in its path and wiping out the little mountain shack at the bottom. Well, those kinds of snowballs are not just from cartoons, they're real! They're called *snow rollers*. They are an extreme, strange, and mysterious weather sight! First, of course, there must be snow on the ground, and then conditions must be just right. The snow must be light and just a tiny bit wet and sticky; it can't be heavy snowman-making snow, and it can't be light, flakey powder, either. That's why snow rollers are extremely rare.

Strong, gusty winds pick up the snow and begin to push it along the ground, forming what looks like barrels of snow, sort of like if you

were trying to make a snowman, except the wind does it. But, unlike the cartoon version, once in motion the rollers tumble on until the wind slackens, until they grow so large that they become lopsided and fall over, or the ground levels off too much for the wind to propel the snow mass any farther.

Snow rollers are a bit mysterious because they are usually formed at night or early in the morning. You can wake up in the morning, go outside, and see a field or a frozen lake covered with hundreds if not thousands of these little rolls in sizes from bowling balls to barrels, all evenly spaced as if they were made by aliens!

Snow Tornadoes

There are many times you may see what looks like a tornado on a snow-covered mountain—giant whirlwinds, or vortices, that pick up snow and create a massive funnel. Those are the snow version of what's called a *dust devil*. I've seen them while skiing, and for fun and an adrenaline rush, I've even skied through them! They are quite a thrill ride; however, I suggest you avoid them unless you are an expert skier.

Sometimes, the conditions are right for an actual tornado to form over a mountaintop during a blizzard or heavy snowstorm. Up-sloping winds on the mountaintop, big blasts of wind shear, heavy bursts of precipitation, thunder, and lightning, all can provide the same things as in a thunderstorm, only of the frozen variety.

Even though there is not one confirmed report of a tornado actually forming in a snowstorm, once in a while they travel over snow-covered fields and forests, and suck up the snow, making them look like a white tornado. In Utah, on December 2, 1970, a twister came across the Timpanogas Divide, where some 38 inches of snow cover had accumulated. The tornado was powerful enough to snap trees 1 foot in diameter, and to suck snow over 1,000-feet high into its funnel. The tornado looked like it was a solid expanse of white, and had a ghostlike appearance.

Try This at Home!

Looking at Snowflakes

Let's take a look at snowflakes and here's how to do it! This activity is from the Weather Wiz Kids Web site (www.weatherwizkids.com/examining_snowflakes.htm).

MATERIALS:
  Black paper or black fabric
  Magnifying glass

PROCESS:
  Place the black paper or fabric in the freezer for a couple of hours.
  Take the black paper or fabric out of the freezer and put it outside when it's snowing.

Let some snowflakes land on the paper or fabric.

Use the magnifying glass to see the beautiful shapes.

EXPLANATION:

This experiment allows you to see the six-sided snowflakes up close and personal. No two snowflakes are identical, so have fun looking at their different shapes.

Great Snowflake Web Sites >>>>

If you would like to grow your own snowflakes in a bottle, visit this site:

www.its.caltech.edu/~atomic/ snowcrystals/project/project.htm.

Check out this site for other ideas for projects with snow:

www.its.caltech.edu/~atomic/ snowcrystals/kids/kids.htm.

SECTION

4

EXTREME WEATHER!

Zap! Pow! Bang! Ba-da-Boom! Ba-da-Bing! It's Lightning!

When you were in elementary school, you likely heard the story of the great Benjamin Franklin and how he discovered that lightning was electricity by flying a kite in a thunderstorm. It was a remarkable idea—but as it's told in school, it doesn't seem very smart, which doesn't make sense when you remember that Ben Franklin was a genius and inventor. Franklin knew that his experiment had to be done— and done as safely as possible—if he wanted to prove his theories about lightning and electricity.

In June 1752 Franklin, with the aid of his son, flew a kite in a

thunderstorm. Franklin tied a key to his end of the silk kite string and tied the string to a post. Many people believe that the key was struck by lightning, but that's not true. On an episode of *MythBusters*, the crew reproduced Franklin's experiment and concluded that if the key had been hit by lightning, Ben Franklin would have been killed.

Instead, Franklin used the kite, key, and silk thread to collect an electric charge from a storm cloud. As the silk became wet from the rain; the string became a great conductor of electricity. Franklin put his hand next to the string and could feel the static from the electric charge of the storm cloud.

Ben Franklin went on to invent the lightning rod, which we still use today to protect homes, businesses, and other buildings.

Other people weren't as smart about electricity as Franklin. The very next year, 1753, a Russian scientist, Georg Richmann, set out to prove that he knew electricity better than Franklin. During a demonstration of ball lightning at a science exposition in St. Petersburg, Russia, Richmann replicated Franklin's experiment, flying a kite in a storm. He didn't use a key; instead, Richmann tied the kite string to the metal box he was standing next to.

When the electrical charge ran down the wet string, it filled the metal box with electricity—which zapped Richmann and killed him!

Lightning is very cool and beautiful, yet powerful and destructive. The leader bolt of lightning can reach a temperature of 54,000°F (29,982.2°C), which is nearly twice the temperature of the sun. If lightning strikes a beach, it can fuse the sand into glass. Sometimes, while digging in a garden, you may find a long piece of a mineral that's green, gray, and white. It's called *fulgurite*, and it's created when a lightning bolt melts soil into a glasslike state.

Even though we know that lightning is caused by electrical charges in a cloud, how those charges get ramped up still remains a mystery. Lightning can also occur within ash clouds from volcanic eruptions, and can be caused by violent forest fires, which generate sufficient dust to create a static charge. The launching of the Space Shuttle and other rockets from Cape Canaveral causes lightning as well.

When you drink sugary soda or eat lots of candy or other sweets, you're likely to feel a burst of extreme uncontrolled energy—a "big charge." That's lightning . . . except lightning needs water and ice crystals to work its magic. Most lightning occurs within a cloud or between a cloud and the ground. Oddly enough, even though a bolt's temperature is hotter than the surface of the sun, lightning only forms in clouds that contain large amounts of ice crystals. The melting and freezing of the ice creates massive electrical charges in the cloud.

There can be lightning in a snowstorm. In March 1996, during a blizzard in Minnesota, a man was struck by lightning and lived. He was dazed and confused, but alive!

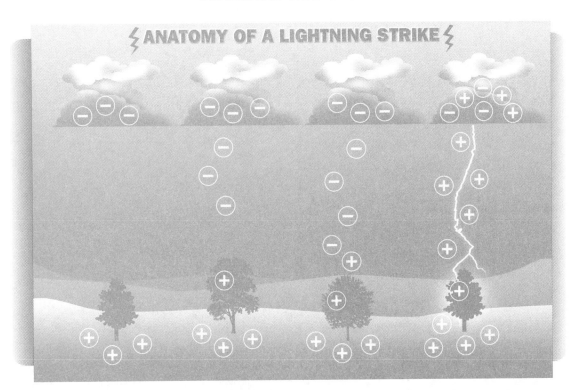

ANATOMY OF A LIGHTNING STRIKE

During a thunderstorm, turbulence in a cloud causes electrical charges to separate. Positive charges rise to the top of the cloud and negative charges fall to the base. Then, because like charges repel, just as magnets do, some of the negative charges on the ground are pushed down, leaving a positive charge on the Earth's surface.

Since opposite charges attract, the positive charges on the ground and the negative charges in the cloud are pulled toward each other, and lightning forms. The first visible lighting stroke is called the *stepped leader*.

When the negative and positive parts of the stepped leader connect, a conductive path is created between the cloud and the ground, and an electrical current begins flowing. Negative charges rush down the path, causing the lightning stroke. After contact, the return stroke begins. This is a blast of positive charge that is traveling upward at about 60,000 miles per second (one-third the speed of light). This is the brilliant light that you see.

What's really cool is when the process repeats several times along the same path, making the lightning

flicker. It all takes place in about half a second!

Lightning is so brilliant that it looks like it is hundreds of yards or even miles wide. Not so! The width of lightning is the size of your pencil!

Hey Ben! Why Don't You Go Fly a Kite?!

HOW BENJAMIN FRANKLIN MADE HIS KITE

From a letter written by Ben Franklin to Peter Collinson, a fellow of the Royal Society, on October 19, 1752:

Make a small cross of two light strips of cedar, the arms so long as to reach to the four corners of a large thin silk handkerchief when extended; tie the corners of the handkerchief to the extremities of the cross, so you have the body of a kite; which being properly accommodated with a tail, loop, and string, will rise in the air, like those made of paper; but this being of silk is fitter to bear the wind and wet of a thunder gust without tearing. To the top of the upright stick of the cross is to be fixed a very sharp pointed wire, rising a foot or more above the wood. To the end of the twine, next the hand, is to be ty'ed a silk ribbon, and where the silk and twine join, a key may be fastened.

This kite is to be raised when a thunder gust appears to be coming on, and the person who holds the string must stand within a door, or window, or under some cover, so that the silk ribbon may not be wet; and care must be taken that the twine does not touch the frame of the door or window. As soon as any of the thunder clouds come over the kite, the pointed wire will draw the electric fire from them, and the kite, with all the twine will be electrified, and the loose filaments of the twine will stand out every way, and be attracted by an approaching finger. And when the rain has wet the kite and twine, so that it can conduct the electric fire freely, you will find it stream out plentifully from the key on the approach of your knuckle. At this key the phial may be charged; and from electric fire thus obtained, spirits may be kindled, and all the other electric experiments be performed, which are usually done by the help of a rubbed glass globe or tube, and thereby the sameness of the electric matter with that of lightning completely demonstrated.

Make Ben's kite! Go to www.pbs .org/benfranklin/

The Thunder from Down Under, Up, and All Around!

When I was a child, I was deathly afraid of booming thunder. To soothe me and to calm my nerves, my parents would try to take my mind off it by saying silly things like, "It's just God moving furniture," or "It's God rolling watermelons under the bed," or my favorite, "It's just the angels bowling!" Fear of thunder is known as *brontophobia* or as I like to put it, "I just feel safer hiding under my bed!" Astraphobia, brontophobia, keraunophobia, and tonitrophobia—all are abnormal fears of lightning and thunder. (I suffer from "Gagaphobia," which is the fear of Lady Gaga!)

Thunder is the result of lightning. Thunder could not exist without lightning. It's obvious when you see lightning that first you see the flash and then you hear the thunder. Experiencing lightning and thunder is one of the easiest ways for people to understand that sound travels much more slowly than light.

Thunder can be heard up to 15 miles away from a lightning strike.

Ever notice how dogs behave when they hear thunder? They hide, or whine, or bark and run around like crazy. My dog, Sandy, barks like mad! I don't know why dogs are affected like this, but if I find out, I'll let you know!

Save Me from This Madness!

Lightning blasts the ground 20 to 30 million times a year. The top six places people get zapped:

1. standing in an open field
2. underneath a tree

3. on bodies of water (boating and fishing)
4. near tractors and other heavy equipment
5. on golf courses

6. on the phone (excluding cell phones and cordless)

How can you stay safe? Get inside a building, or inside a car or truck with the windows closed!

You can survive being struck by lightning—in fact, the majority of people who are struck do not die. This definitely does *not* mean that you should ignore the danger and stay outside during a storm!

Your chance of surviving a lightning strike is greater if someone nearby knows CPR. Unlike the cartoons, lightning does not blow up a person, cause someone to burst into flames, or fry anyone into a smoldering black lump! Lightning can burn off your hair or singe your clothes, but mostly it affects your body's electrical system.

Most people who are struck by lightning appear dead, but they are in cardiac arrest and need CPR. Many people think that if you touch someone who has been struck by lightning, you will get electrocuted. That only happens in cartoons! There is no danger in touching or aiding someone who has been struck by lightning.

If you are outside during a thunderstorm and you feel your hair start to stand on end, or if you're fishing and your line appears to just hang in the air when you cast, or if you are wearing a raincoat that feels like it's lifting into the air, lightning will strike soon. You are feeling the static electrical charges in the air mounting. Get to a place of safety immediately!

There's electricity in the air!

This Dude Is 'da Man! The Story of Roy Sullivan

"Lightning set my underclothes on fire!" said Roy Sullivan to a captivated audience on the 1980s TV show, *That's Incredible!* Roy was a ranger in the Shenandoah National Park in the Blue Ridge Mountains of Virginia. He was dubbed the "human lightning rod." He had been stuck by lightning eight times. That's right, in eight separate incidents he was struck by lightning and lived! Roy owns a place in the *Guinness Book of World Records* for being struck by lightning more than any other human being.

The first hit he took was while he was standing in the park's lookout tower in 1942. His only injury was the loss of a big toenail. In 1969, Roy's eyebrows were singed when lightning struck him while he was driving along a mountain road. A year later he was walking across his yard when lightning zapped him again, searing his left shoulder.

In 1972, he was struck a fourth time while working in the ranger station. The lightning set his hair on fire! He grabbed a bucket of water and poured it over his head to put out the flames. "I'm just allergic to lightning," he said at the time.

While on patrol in the Shenandoah National Park in 1973, Roy saw a storm cloud forming and drove away quickly. He said the cloud seemed to follow him. He thought he had outrun it, but when he got out of his truck, lightning struck him for the fifth time and left him with an injured ankle.

Just when you thought his luck might turn for the better, it got worse! While fishing in a fresh-water pond on a Saturday morning in 1977, lightning struck Roy for the seventh time, hitting him in the top of the head and traveling down his right side. With his hair singed and burns on his chest and stomach, Roy staggered toward his car. As he stumbled down the trail, a bear appeared and tried to swipe three trout from his fishing line! Despite everything that had happened, Roy managed to find the courage and strength to smack the bear with a branch. That was the twenty-second bear he had hit in his lifetime.

In the early 1980s, Roy Sullivan was struck by lightning for the eighth time. Roy just seemed to attract lightning. But despite the number of times he was zapped, he was never seriously hurt! He believed that an unseen force was trying to destroy him. He told a reporter once, "I don't believe God is after me. If he were, the first bolt would have been enough."

Oddly enough, Roy lived in a town named Dooms!

If I were as lucky as Roy, I would have bought a lottery ticket!

A CLASSIC LITERARY MOMENT

One blinding flash after another came, and peal on peal of deafening thunder. And now a drenching rain poured down and the rising hurricane drove it in sheets along the ground. The boys cried out to each other, but the roaring wind and the booming thunderblasts drowned their voices utterly.

—Mark Twain,
The Adventures of Tom Sawyer

Holy Cow! It's Raining Lightning!

Lightning takes many different forms and shapes. All lightning discharges occur in the same manner, but the conditions under which they develop and are viewed make the flash look different. Scientists and ordinary people have given different types of lighting interesting names, such as:

Andes Lightning
Anvil Crawler
Ball Lightning
Band Lightning
Beaded Lightning
Black Lightning
Blue Jet
Chain Lightning
Cloud-to-Air Lightning
Cloud-to-Cloud Lightning

Cloud-to-Ground Lightning
Corona Discharge
Dry Lightning
Fillet Lightning
Forked Lightning
Globe Lightning

Heat Lightning
Pearl Lightning
Ribbon Lightning
Rocket Lightning
Sheet Lightning
Sprite
Stellar Lightning
St. Elmo's Fire
Streak Lightning
Thunderbolt
Zigzag Lightning

Did you know the speed of light is 186,000 miles per second? I wonder how fast lightning would be if it didn't zigzag!!

Could Someone Please, Please, Give Me a Glass of Water?— Drought

Droughts are extremely prolonged weather events that cause severe environmental, economic, and sociological damage. A drought is simply a long period—a season or

Kangaroo in drought conditions

more—of dry weather. During a drought, there is either no precipitation or much, much less than normal. Droughts can last for months, or even years.

Unlike wet weather events like thunderstorms and hurricanes, which have a somewhat predictable life cycle and timetable, there is no certain time that a drought begins or ends. The most famous droughts in U.S. history occurred in the 1930s, at the same time as a massive heat wave. These two conditions created one of the greatest and most devastating weather disasters ever. And to top it all off, this happened at the time of the Great Depression, when the U.S. economy was at an all-time low.

Poor farming practices and years of sustained drought were the cause of the Dust Bowl, an area of more than 50 million acres that stretched from Texas to Canada, and from Colorado to Illinois. Farmers deeply plowed the Plains grasslands and planted wheat. Even though the drought continued, farmers kept planting—and nothing grew.

The plants that held the topsoil in place were gone. Windstorms blew that topsoil into rolling clouds of dust, which turned day into night. At one point during 1935, the Texas Panhandle saw 38 days of continuous storms that sent dust all the way from the Great Plains to the East Coast and out to sea. Dust deposits were reported on ships as far as 300 miles from the coast!

A lake during a prolonged drought

Droughts are not a thing of the past. There are droughts going on all over the Earth almost all the time. In 2002, Colorado reported its driest year since record keeping began in 1895. Wildfires, out of control due to parch conditions, burned over a million acres in Arizona and Colorado.

Drought is measured on a scale called the *Palmer Index*.

PALMER DROUGHT SEVERITY INDEX

PALMER INDEX	SOIL MOISTURE
Above +4	Extremely Moist
+3 to +4	Very Moist
+2 to +3	Moist
-2 to +2	Average, Normal
-2 to -3	Dry
-3 to -4	Very Dry
Below -4	Extremely Dry

The positive numbers mean that above-normal soil conditions exist, with +4 being extremely moist. The negative numbers mean that the soil is extremely dry, with -4 being the worst. Negative numbers can lead to devastating conditions.

U.S. Drought Monitor maps are issued weekly by the Climate Prediction Center of NOAA. These maps show areas around the country which are effected by drought. In 2003, states in the Great Plains and in the West experienced one of the worst droughts in 108 years.

ANOTHER CLASSIC LITERARY MOMENT

The Grapes of Wrath by John Steinbeck is one of my favorite books. This is from that classic 1939 novel:

And then the dispossessed were drawn west—from Kansas, Oklahoma, Texas, New Mexico; from Nevada and Arkansas, families, tribes, dusted out, tractored out. Carloads, caravans, homeless and hungry; twenty thousand and fifty thousand and a hundred thousand and two hundred thousand. They streamed over the mountains, hungry and restless—restless as ants, scurrying to find work to do—to lift, to push, to pull, to pick, to cut—anything, any burden to bear, for food. The kids are hungry. We got no place to live. Like ants scurrying for work, for food, and most of all for land.

Watering restrictions during droughts can lead to "brown lawn."

Someone Please Give Me Some A/C!

Wherever I go, I love to eavesdrop on people who are talking about the weather. One of my favorite topics—besides hearing that meteorologists always get it wrong—is when people compare heat in the eastern United States to the heat in the western United States. They say, "Yeah, but out west, it's a dry heat; in the east, we have the humidity!" The argument that "it's the humidity, not the heat" is pretty much a nonstarter. From June through August, the U.S. Southwest broils in 110°F heat and that's uncomfortably hot no matter what the humidity!

Compare the two charts on page 176. One shows average annual temperature; the other, average temperatures just in July. You'll see a heck of a difference!

FIFTEEN HOTTEST MAJOR CITIES IN THE UNITED STATES— AVERAGE ANNUAL TEMPERATURES, 1970–2000

LOCATION	TEMPERATURE
Key West, FL	78.0°F (25.6°C)
Honolulu, HI	77.5°F (25.3°C)
Miami, FL	76.6°F (24.8°C)
Fort Lauderdale, FL	75.7°F (24.3°C)
West Palm Beach, FL	75.3°F (24.1°C)
Fort Myers, FL	74.9°F (23.8°C)
Yuma, AZ	74.6°F (23.7°C)
Hilo, HI	74.1°F (23.4°C)
St. Petersburg, FL	74.1°F (23.4°C)
Brownsville, TX	74.0°F (23.3°C)
Phoenix, AZ	73.9°F (23.3°C)
Palm Springs, CA	73.8°F (23.2°C)
Laredo, TX	73.7°F (23.2°C)
Orlando, FL	72.7°F (22.6°C)
Corpus Christi, TX	72.1°F (22.3°C)

FIFTEEN HOTTEST MAJOR CITIES IN THE UNITED STATES— AVERAGE JULY MAXIMUM TEMPERATURES, 1970–2000

LOCATION	TEMPERATURE
Palm Springs, CA	108.3°F (42.4°C)
Yuma, AZ	107.0°F (41.7°C)
Phoenix, AZ	106.0°F (41.1°C)
Las Vegas, NV	104.1°F (40.1°C)
Tucson, AZ	101.0°F (38.3°C)
Presidio, TX	100.6°F (38.1°C)
Laredo, TX	100.5°F (38.1°C)
Redding, CA	99.5°F (37.5°C)
Bakersfield, CA	98.2°F (36.8°C)
Fresno, CA	98.1°F (36.7°C)
Wichita Falls, TX	97.6°F (36.4°C)
Waco, TX	96.7°F (35.9°C)
Dallas–Ft. Worth, TX	96.3°F (35.7°C)
Del Rio, TX	96.2°F (35.7°C)
El Paso, TX	95.5°F (35.3°C)

That's Why It's Called Death Valley!

Death Valley is the hottest place in the world! No one will live there until someone comes up with an operation to replace your appendix with central air-conditioning. It is located in southern California, and has the most extreme heat of any area on Earth! Imagine a vast expanse of sand, littered with animal bones—with maybe some human ones thrown in—and, well, you get the picture.

Death Valley's maximum temperature of 134°F (56.7°C), recorded on July 10, 1913, is the hottest temperature ever recorded in the Western Hemisphere. That temperature is surpassed by only one other city in the world: Al Aziziyah, Libya, which once recorded a temperature of 136.4°F (57.8°C) on September 22, 1922.

What makes Death Valley unique is that it's consistently hot. The longest stretch of consecutive days with a maximum of 100°F (37.8°C) or higher was 154 days in 2001. This is only eclipsed by Marble Bar, West Australia, which had a run of 161 consecutive days with highs of 100°F (37.8°C) or more in 1923–1924.

July 2006 was Death Valley's hottest month on record: the average temperature was 106°F (41°C)! And on July 19, 2005, the temperature ranged from a low of 101°F (38°C) to a high of 129°F (54°C), meaning the daily average was 115°F (46°C). That's likely to be the hottest average daily temperature ever recorded anywhere in the world.

What did one skeleton lying in Death Valley say to the other? "It's not the heat, it's the humidity!"

Putting ice down your pants sounds like a good idea about now!

Is My State the Warmest, or Just Very Friendly?

(Annual Maximum July Temperatures from 1971–2000)

STATE	TEMPERATURE	LOCATION
Alabama	93.6°F (34.2°C)	Bessemer
Alaska	73.9°F (26.3°C)	Central
Arizona	112.5°F (44.7°C)	Willow Beach
Arkansas	94.7°F (34.8°C)	Blue Mountain Dam
California	114.9°F (46.1°C)	Death Valley
Colorado	94.9°F (34.9°C)	Uravan
Connecticut	85.4°F (29.7°C)	Stamford
Delaware	87.6°F (30.9°C)	Newark
Florida	94.7°F (34.8°C)	Lakeland
Georgia	94.7°F (34.8°C)	Waycross
Hawaii	88.9°F (31.6°C)	Honolulu
Idaho	91.2°F (32.9°C)	Glenns Ferry
Illinois	91.2°F (32.9°C)	Kaskaskia River Lock
Indiana	90.5°F (32.5°C)	Evansville
Iowa	88.3°F (31.3°C)	Keosauqua
Kansas	95.9°F (35.5°C)	Wilmore
Kentucky	93.6°F (34.2°C)	Gilbertsville Dam
Louisiana	94.5°F (34.7°C)	Calhoun Research Station

STATE	TEMPERATURE	LOCATION
Maine	82.5°F (28.1°C)	Sanford
Maryland	90.6°F (32.6°C)	Baltimore
Massachusetts	85.5°F (29.7°C)	Chester
Michigan	85.7°F (29.8°C)	Dearborn
Minnesota	85.5°F (29.7°C)	Chaska
Mississippi	93.0°F (33.9°C)	Belzoni
Missouri	92.8°F (33.8°C)	Kennett
Montana	91.5°F (33.1°C)	Brandenburg
Nebraska	93.3°F (34.1°C)	Beaver City
Nevada	108.4°F (42.4°C)	Laughlin
New Hampshire	83.2°F (28.4°C)	Durham
New Jersey	88.1°F (31.2°C)	Woodtown
New Mexico	91.1°F (32.8°C)	Lordsburg
New York	86.0°F (30.0°C)	Scarsdale
North Carolina	86.2°F (30.1°C)	Whiteville
North Dakota	86.2°F (30.1°C)	Medora
Ohio	88.1°F (31.2°C)	Fairfield
Oklahoma	98.6°F (37.0°C)	Chattanooga
Oregon	95.4°F (35.2°C)	Pelton Dam
Pennsylvania	87.6°F (30.9°C)	Hanover
Rhode Island	82.6°F (28.1°C)	Providence
South Carolina	95.2°F (35.1°C)	Columbia (Univ. of SC)
South Dakota	91.9°F (33.3°C)	Fort Pierre
Tennessee	92.1°F (33.4°C)	Memphis
Texas	103.4°F (39.7°C)	Castolon
Utah	102.8°F (39.3°C)	St. George
Vermont	83.8°F (28.8°C)	Vernon
Virginia	91.1°F (32.8°C)	Stony Creek
Washington	91.0°F (32.8°C)	Smyrna
West Virginia	89.4°F (31.9°C)	Williamson
Wisconsin	85.6°F (29.8°C)	Lake Geneva
Wyoming	90.7°F (32.6°C)	Whalen

You Are on Fiiiiiiiiirrrrrrrre!! All-Time Record Highs

STATE	TEMPERATURE	LOCATION
Alabama	112°F (44°C)	Centerville
Alaska	100°F (38°C)	Fort Yukon
Arizona	128°F (53°C)	Lake Havasu City
Arkansas	120°F (49°C)	Ozark
California	134°F (57°C)	Death Valley
Colorado	118°F (48°C)	Bennett
Connecticut	106°F (41°C)	Danbury
Delaware	110°F (43°C)	Millsboro
Florida	109°F (43°C)	Monticello
Georgia	112°F (44°C)	Greenville
Hawaii	100°F (38°C)	Pahala
Idaho	118°F (48°C)	Orofino
Illinois	117°F (47°C)	East St. Louis
Indiana	116°F (47°C)	Collegeville
Iowa	118°F (48°C)	Keokuk
Kansas	121°F (49°C)	Alton
Kentucky	114°F (46°C)	Greensburg
Louisiana	114°F (46°C)	Plain Dealing
Maine	105°F (41°C)	North Bridgton
Maryland	109°F (43°C)	Cumberland
Massachusetts	107°F (42°C)	New Bedford
Michigan	112°F (44°C)	Mio
Minnesota	114°F (46°C)	Moorhead

STATE	TEMPERATURE	LOCATION
Mississippi	115°F (46°C)	Holly Springs
Missouri	118°F (48°C)	Warsaw
Montana	117°F (47°C)	Medicine Lake
Nebraska	118°F (48°C)	Minden
Nevada	125°F (52°C)	Laughlin
New Hampshire	106°F (41°C)	Nashua
New Jersey	110°F (43°C)	Runyon
New Mexico	122°F (50°C)	Waste ISO Plant
New York	108°F (42°C)	Troy
North Carolina	110°F (43°C)	Fayetteville
North Dakota	121°F (49°C)	Steele
Ohio	113°F (45°C)	Gallipolis
Oklahoma	120°F (49°C)	Tipton
Oregon	119°F (48°C)	Pendleton
Pennsylvania	111°F (44°C)	Phoenixville
Rhode Island	104°F (40°C)	Providence
South Carolina	111°F (44°C)	Camden
South Dakota	120°F (49°C)	Usta
Tennessee	113°F (45°C)	Perryville
Texas	120°F (49°C)	Seymour
Utah	117°F (47°C)	St. George
Vermont	105°F (41°C)	Vernon
Virginia	110°F (43°C)	Balcony Falls
Washington	118°F (48°C)	Ice Harbor Dam
West Virginia	112°F (44°C)	Martinsburg
Wisconsin	114°F (46°C)	Wisconsin Dells
Wyoming	115°F (46°C)	Basin

It's Blow-Torchin', Flame-Throwin' Hot!— World Record High Temperatures

COUNTRY	TEMPERATURE	LOCATION
Africa		
Libya	136.4°F (58.0°C)*	Al Aziziyah
Algeria	135°F (57°C)	Tindouf
Egypt	124°F (51°C)	Aswan
Morocco	122°F (50°C)	Quazartzate
Niger	122°F (50°C)	Agadez
Ethiopia	121°F (49°C)	Dallol
Mozambique	120°F (49°C)	Zumboa
Senegal	120°F (49°C)	Matam and Kaolak
Namibia	118°F (48°C)	Noordoewer
Zimbabwe	117°F (47°C)	Beitbridge
Cameroon	115°F (46°C)	Maroua
Swaziland	115°F (46°C)	Dearn
Botswana	111°F (44°C)	Gabarone and Ghanzi
Sierra Leone	111°F (44°C)	Kabala
Angola	110°F (43°C)	Dondo
Canary Islands	109°F (43°C)	Santa Cruz
Liberia	109°F (43°C)	Sagleipie
Cape Verde	108°F (42°C)	Praia
Kenya	105°F (41°C)	Garissa
Tanzania	103°F (39°C)	Moshi

*Hottest official temperature recorded in the world, September 22, 1922

COUNTRY	TEMPERATURE	LOCATION
Rwanda	96°F (36°C)	Kigali

North America

United States	134°F (57°C)	Death Valley, CA
Mexico	124°F (51°C)	Mexicali
Canada	113°F (45°C)	Midale and Yellow Grass, SK
Cuba	108°F (42°C)	Sagua de Tanamo
Greenland	86°F (30°C)	Ivigtut

Asia

Israel	129°F (54°C)	Tirat Tsvi
Iran	128.3°F (53.5°C)	Ahwaz
Pakistan	127°F (53°C)	Jacobabdad
Iraq	126°F (52°C)	Ash Shu'aybah
Kuwait	125°F (52°C)	Kuwait City
Saudi Arabia	125°F (52°C)	Abaiq
Afghanistan	124°F (51°C)	Zaranj
India	123°F (51°C)	Alwar
China	121°F (49°C)	Turpan
Jordan	121°F (49°C)	Aqaba
Syria	121°F (49°C)	Hassakah
Kazakhstan	120.5°F (49°C)	Turkestan
Vietnam	109°F (43°C)	Hanoi and Lao Cai
Korea	108°F (42°C)	Chain, S. Korea
Philippines	108°F (42°C)	Tuguegarao
Cambodia	107°F (42°C)	Stoeng Treng
Japan	106°F (41°C)	Yamagata
Malaysia	105°F (41°C)	Chuping

COUNTRY	TEMPERATURE	LOCATION
Sri Lanka	104°F (40°C)	Anuradhapura
Singapore	100°F (38°C)	Paya Lebar

Oceania and the Poles

COUNTRY	TEMPERATURE	LOCATION
Australia	123.3°F (50.7°C)	Oodnadatta
New Zealand	108°F (42°C)	Rangiora and Jordan
Antarctica	59.3°F (15°C)	Bases Orcadas and Marambio South Pole
North Pole	39°F (4°C)	North Pole

Europe

COUNTRY	TEMPERATURE	LOCATION
Portugal	123°F (51°C)	Los Riodades
Spain	122°F (50°C)	Seville
Italy	119°F (48°C)	Catenanuovo, Sicily
France	111.5°F (44.2°C)	Conqueyrac
Russia	109°F (43°C)	Elista
Hungary	108°F (42°C)	Bekescsaba
Switzerland	106.7°F (41.5°C)	Grono
Germany	104.5°F (40.3°C)	Perl-Nenning
Poland	104°F (40°C)	Prószków
Austria	103.5°F (39.7°C)	Dellach im Drautal
Belgium	102°F (39°C)	Haacht
Holland	101.5°F (38.6°C)	Warnsveld
Great Britain	101.3°F (38.5°C)	Brogdale
Sweden	100.4°F (38°C)	Ultuna, & Malilla
Denmark	98°F (37°C)	Holstebro
Finland	97°F (36°C)	Turku
Norway	96.1°F (35.6°C)	Nesbyen

COUNTRY	TEMPERATURE	LOCATION
South and Central America		
Argentina	120.4°F (49.1°C)	Villa de Maria
Bolivia	117°F (47°C)	Villa Montes
Brazil	113°F (45°C)	Bom Jesus do Piaui
Paraguay	113°F (45°C)	Pedro Pena
Uruguay	113°F (45°C)	Melo
El Salvador	112.5°F (44.7°C)	San Miquel
Guatemala	111°F (44°C)	La Fragua
Honduras	111°F (44°C)	San Pedro Sula
Venezuela	109.5°F (43.1°C)	Guanare
Colombia	109°F (43°C)	Barrancabermeja
Costa Rica	108°F (42°C)	Puntarenas
Peru	108°F (42°C)	Pucallpa
Nicaragua	107.5°F (41.9°C)	Chinandega
Chile	107°F (41°C)	Los Angeles
Ecuador	104°F (40°C)	San Lorenzo
Panama	104°F (40°C)	San Francisco

Sandblasted and Dusted Off!!

A sandstorm or dust storm is a wild meteorological phenomenon. In the Sudan a sandstorm is called a *haboob*. In the Sahara, a *simoom*. The term *sandstorm* is most often used to describe desert sandstorms where the sand is blown about close to the surface. The term *dust storm* is usually used when finer particles are blown for long distances. Dust storms are generally associated with urban areas.

Both kinds of storms occur when the air is very dry and the winds are strong enough to loosen sand or dust from the surface of the ground. The wind carries away the sand and dust, eroding the soil in one place and depositing it in another.

A sandstorm can move whole sand dunes. A dust storm can carry such large amounts of dust that it can reach a mile high. Levels of Saharan dust coming off the east coast of Africa in 2007 were the highest since 1999. This was enough dust to cool the Atlantic waters, reducing the amount of hurricanes that normally would be produced in that area.

Dust storms have a huge negative economic impact in areas where they remove soil full of nutrient-rich particles, reducing food production. However, dust storms can also be beneficial. In Central and South America, the rain forests get their nutrients from the Sahara. Plus, dust in Hawaii increases plant growth. "I would hang ten, but I've got these plants growing all over my surfboard, dude!"

The Answer, My Friend, Is Blowin' in the Wind

This is an account written by Vance Johnson, who witnessed a dust storm in western Kansas in the 1930s:

The darkness was dust. The windows turned solid pitch; even flower boxes six inches beyond the pane were shut from view. Dust sifted into houses, through cracks around the doors and windows—so thick even in well-built homes a man in a chair across the room became a blurred outline. Sparks flew between pieces of metal and men got a shock when they touched the plumbing. It hurt to breathe, but a damp cloth held over mouth and nose helped for a while. Food on tables freshly set for dinner was ruined. Milk turned black. Bed, rugs, furniture, clothes in closets, and food in the refrigerator were covered with a film of dust. Its acrid odor came out of pillows for days afterward.

What the Hail Is That?

Those really nice warm days of summer can turn out some really nice-size thunderstorms that produce not only torrents of rain, wind, lightning, and tornadoes, but also hail. Yes, ice that falls from the sky, sometimes in amazing sizes. There's pea-, dime-, quarter-, golf ball-, baseball-, and grapefruit-size hail. My favorite is canned-ham size!

That's big!

Hail is not to be confused with sleet. The easiest way to remember the difference is that hail falls in the summer and sleet falls in the winter. Sleet is also a lot smaller than hail.

Hail is formed in spring and summer from tremendous cumulonimbus clouds known as thunderheads. Cumulonimbus clouds harbor a vast amount of energy in the form of updrafts and downdrafts. These vertical winds can reach speeds of over 110 mph. Hail grows in the main updraft, where most of the cloud is formed of what's called "supercooled" water. This is water that remains liquid although its temperature is at or below freezing (32°F/0°C). A supercooled water drop remains liquid until it encounters something solid on which it can freeze. Ice crystals, frozen raindrops, dust, and salt from the ocean are also present in the cloud. Supercooled water will freeze onto any of these hosts, creating a hailstone or enlarging hailstones that already exist.

Hailstones are usually formed in layers as they bounce around inside the cloud, with supercooled water accumulating and freezing at different rates in different locations. The more supercooled water a hailstone comes in contact with, the larger and heavier the stone is likely to become. When the hailstone becomes so heavy that the updraft can no longer support it, it falls from the sky.

Hail falls along paths called hail swaths, which vary in size from a few square acres to 10 miles wide and even 100 miles long. Hail can accumulate in piles so deep it has to be removed by a snowplow! In Orient, Iowa, in August 1980, hail drifts were reported to be 6 feet (2 meters) deep. On July 11, 1990, softball-size hail fell in Denver, Colorado, and caused $625 million in damage, mostly to automobiles and the roofs of buildings. Forty-seven people at an amusement park were seriously injured when a power failure trapped them on a Ferris wheel and they were battered by softball-size hail.

Hail causes a tremendous amount of crop damage worldwide. It can shred crops in a matter of minutes. In the United States alone, the cost runs into hundreds of millions of dollars a year. Farmers offset this by buying crop insurance. Illinois farmers buy more crop insurance than anyone else, spending $600 million each year. However, hail is most common in an area called *hail alley*, where Colorado, Wyoming, and Nebraska meet.

Hail is being battled around the world by a technique called *cloud seeding*. Insurance companies, as well as cities and countries around the world, have been using cloud seeding to save crops and property. The practice is very common in China, where feeding the country's large population has forced the nation's leaders to turn to cloud seeding to lessen crop damage caused by hail.

You're Using Seeds to Grow Clouds? What Are You Trying to Make, a Chia Cloud?

What is cloud seeding? I have seen it done and I can tell you it's very cool. An airplane flies into storm clouds during a severe thunderstorm. This is very dangerous as the plane has to fly right into the lower layers of the thunderstorm to perform its work. The tremendous downdrafts of the storm, also known as wind shear, could push the aircraft right into the ground, so the pilot has to be very careful!

Attached to the aircraft's wings are flares. They look something like roadway flares or Roman candles.

Inside the flares is a chemical called *silver iodide.*

Flying in the teeth of the storm, the plane drops millions of silver iodide smoke particles. The particles act as artificial ice crystals and freeze the water drops in the storm's updraft. In hail storms, the rapid formation of cloud water occurs in the lower part of the cloud. When this exceeds the rate of natural ice crystal growth, it creates an environment ripe for hail. The billions of ice crystals formed from seeding freeze the supercooled water, which results in the storm producing smaller, less dangerous hailstones.

The thousands of ice crystals made from the silver iodide smoke particles will start to crystallize using up the liquid water so that water isn't available for hail to grow to large size. The more water used to make ice crystals means less water left to form larger hailstones.

St. Louis, Missouri, is the number one site of hail damage in the United States with a record $1.9 billion. Calgary, Alberta, Canada, began an aggressive cloud-seeding program after a 30-minute hailstorm in 1991 caused a record 116,000 insurance claims to be filed, resulting in a payout of what today would be $1 billion. With populations growing and property values skyrocketing, cloud seeding has become a very cost-effective way to battle hail!

I'm Going Down, Down, Down, in a Burning Ring of Fire!—or, Shake It, Shake It, Baby!

Did you know that 80 percent of the planet's earthquakes occur along the rim of the Pacific Ocean, in an area called the Ring of Fire? This zone runs along the west coast of South, Central, and North America, from the tip of the southern continent through the Aleutian Islands, and then continues to circle the Pacific Ocean along the eastern coast of Asia, south to Japan and the Philippines, then farther south around the eastern side of Australia to New Zealand, for a total distance of roughly 50,000 miles. The Ring of Fire is home to 452 volcanoes—that's 75 percent of the world's active and dormant volcanoes.

I'm sure you're familiar with the basics of an earthquake, the tremendous shaking of the ground

Earthquake damage in Turkey

tectonics. In some places, the plates rub against each other; in others, one plate sinks beneath another; and still in others, the plates shift away from each other.

When any of these things happen, the usual smooth movement of the plates is disrupted. Sometimes, plates become jammed together at their edges while the rest of the plate continues to move. The rocks along the edges of the plates become distorted with what in earthquake lingo is called a *strain* as the plates flex. Over time, the strain builds up to the point where the rock cannot bend anymore. With a lurch, the rock breaks and the two plates move. An earthquake is the shaking that radiates out from the breaking rock.

The San Andreas Fault in California marks one place where the giant rock plates rub against each other. In 1906, the release of strain caused the Great San Francisco Earthquake. The quake, the aftershocks, and the fires triggered by the tremors, which burned for three days, killed somewhere between 700 and 3,000 people. That is the largest death toll ever for an

that is caused by an abrupt shift of rock along a fracture in the Earth, called a *fault*. Earthquakes usually last no longer than 30 to 40 seconds. But in those few seconds, an earthquake releases stress that may have been accumulating within the rock for hundreds of years.

Scientists believe that most earthquakes are caused by slow movements inside the Earth that push against the Earth's brittle, relatively thin outer layer, causing rocks to break suddenly. These are not rocks you can put in your hand, but gigantic rocks that take up many hundreds of square miles!

The surface of the Earth is covered with immense, large, rigid plates of rock, which move slowly and continually in response to the flow of molten rock within the Earth. The study of this motion is called *plate*

Earthquake damage in California

earthquake in the United States.

The size of an earthquake is indicated by a number called its *magnitude.* Magnitude is calculated

A view of San Francisco after the 1906 earthquake.

from a measurement of either the strength or the length of time of recorded *seismic waves,* or what I like to call the "shake, rattle, and roll." Magnitude is determined from

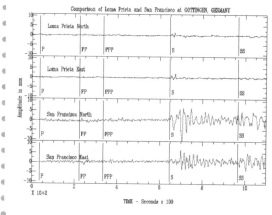

measurements made from seismograms and not on reports of the shaking or interpretations of building damage. (This is different from the Fujita scale described in the chapter about tornadoes, which is based solely on the damage to buildings and other structures.)

Who Moved My Plate?

The rates of plate movement range from about three-quarters of an inch to 4.5 inches per year. That movement can be measured by precise ground-surveying techniques using laser-electronic instruments. Global Positioning System (GPS) has been very useful for studying the shifts in the Earth's crust. Twenty-one satellites are currently in orbit 13,777 miles above the Earth as part of the NAVSTAR system of the U.S. Department of Defense. These satellites continuously transmit radio signals back to Earth. To determine its precise position on Earth (longitude, latitude, elevation), each GPS ground site must simultaneously receive signals from at least four satellites, recording the exact location of each satellite and the time when its signal was received. By repeatedly measuring distances between specific points, geologists can determine if there has been active movement along faults or between plates. The separations between GPS sites are already being measured regularly around the Pacific basin.

"Yo, Plates, We'll Be Watching YOU!"

Deadliest Earthquakes of All Time!

DATE	LOCATION	DEATHS	MAGNITUDE
January 23, 1556	Shansi, China	830,000	~8
July 27, 1976	Tangshan, China	255,000	7.5
August 9, 1138	Aleppo, Syria	230,000	n.a.
December 26, 2004	West coast, North Sumatra	225,000+	9.0
December 22, 856*	Damghan, Iran	200,000	n.a.
May 22, 1927	near Xining, Tsinghai, China	200,000	7.9
December 16, 1920	Gansu, China	200,000	7.8
March 23, 893*	Ardabil, Iran	150,000	n.a.
September 1, 1923	Kwanto, Japan	143,000	7.9
October 5, 1948	Ashgabat, Turkmenistan, USSR	110,000	7.3
September 1290	Chihli, China	100,000	n.a.
December 28, 1908	Messina, Italy	70,000–100,000	7.2
October 8, 2005	Pakistan	80,361	7.6
November 1667	Shemakha, Caucasia	80,000	n.a.
November 18, 1727	Tabriz, Iran	77,000	n.a.
December 25, 1932	Gansu, China	70,000	7.6
November 1, 1755	Lisbon, Portugal	70,000	8.7
May 31, 1970	Peru	66,000	7.9
January 11, 1693	Sicily, Italy	60,000	n.a.
1268	Silicia, Asia Minor	60,000	n.a.
May 30, 1935	Quetta, Pakistan	30,000–60,000	7.5
June 20, 1990	Iran	50,000	7.7
February 4, 1783	Calabria, Italy	50,000	n.a.

*These dates are prior to 1000 CE.

Dude, Take It from "Tommy Tsunami," You Do *Not* Want to Catch *That* Wave!

It's very exciting to sit at the beach on a sunny blue-sky day and watch giant waves come crashing ashore. I love watching surfers try to keep those great monster waves from swallowing them. Laird Hamilton is my favorite surfer. He's extremely cool when it comes to riding gigantic waves that are five to eight stories high, shooting the curl on his board at up to 80 mph. However, the waves Laird and his surfer pals ride look nothing like the real killer of a wave called a *tsunami*. Most people who have not experienced a tsunami imagine that it looks like one of those towering, surfable waves with a giant curl. But that's not what a tsunami looks like.

A tsunami is a series of huge waves that occur as the result of a violent underwater disturbance such as an earthquake or a volcanic eruption. The waves travel in all directions from the epicenter of the disturbance, much like the ripples that happen when a rock is thrown into a pond. The waves may travel in the open sea as fast as 450 mph. In the open ocean, tsunami waves are not generally large—hence the difficulty in detecting the approach of a tsunami. In the open ocean, they would not even be felt by ships because their wavelength is hundreds of miles long with a height of only a few feet. But as these powerful waves approach shallow waters along the coast, their velocity is slowed and the waves swell to a great height before smashing into the shore. Wave heights have been known to reach more than 100 feet (30.5 meters)! Even a wave that is 10 to 20 feet high can cause many deaths or injuries.

The first wave is usually not the largest or most significant wave in the series. Furthermore, one coastal community may experience no

damaging waves while another, not that far away, may be pounded by deadly, destructive waves. Depending on a number of factors, some low-lying areas could experience severe inland flooding of water and debris of more than 1,000 feet.

So Who Is "Sue Nomee"?

Tsunami is the Japanese word for "harbor wave." Tsunamis used to be mistakenly referred to as *tidal waves*, but they have nothing to do with the tides.

The deadliest tsunami in history happened on December 26, 2004, when a 9.0 magnitude earthquake ruptured the floor of the Indian Ocean off the northwest coast of the Indonesian island of Sumatra. The earthquake triggered the deadliest tsunami in world history. More than 225,000 people died from the disaster; thousands were injured, thousands remain missing, and millions were left homeless.

Wave It Good-bye!— Deadliest Tsunamis in History

FATALITIES	YEAR	MAGNITUDE	PRINCIPAL AREA
225,000	2004	9.0	Indian Ocean
110,000	1410 B.C.	n.a	Crete, Ancient Greece
60,000	1755	8.5	Portugal, Morocco
40,000	1782	7.0	South China Sea
36,500	1883	n.a.	Krakatau, Indonesia
30,000	1707	8.4	Tokaido-Nankaido, Japan
26,360	1896	7.6	Sanriku, Japan
25,674	1868	8.5	Northern Chile
15,030	1792	6.4	Kyushu Island, Japan
13,486	1771	7.4	Ryukyu Trench, Japan

How Will I Know If a Tsunami Is Coming?

The National Oceanic and Atmospheric Administration (NOAA) uses many tools to detect an oncoming tsunami. Tsunami warning centers use earthquake information, tide gauges, and a new tool from NOAA—tsunami detection buoys, developed by NOAA's Pacific Marine Environmental Laboratory. Six of these buoys are now deployed in the North Pacific to help scientists determine whether a tsunami has been generated and is heading for North American coastlines. More buoys are needed, however, especially since the buoys can suffer outages in the harsh North Pacific Ocean.

Tsunami Watches and Warnings

Tsunami Warning

A high-level threat. Indicates that a tsunami is imminent and that coastal locations in the warned area should prepare for flooding. The initial warning is typically based on seismic information alone. Earthquakes over magnitude 7.0 trigger a warning covering all coastal regions within 2 hours tsunami travel time from the epicenter. When the magnitude is over 7.5, the warned area is increased to 3 hours tsunami travel time. As water level data showing the tsunami is recorded, the warning will be cancelled, restricted, or expanded as conditions indicate.

Tsunami Watch

A lower-level threat than a tsunami warning. The area included in the watch is based on the magnitude of the earthquake and the borders of the warning zone. For earthquakes over magnitude 7.0, the watch area is 1 hour tsunami travel time outside the warning zone. For earthquakes over magnitude 7.5, the watch area is 3 hours tsunami travel time outside the warning zone. Subsequent bulletins will either upgrade the watch to a warning or cancel it, depending on the severity of the tsunami.

Upon receipt of tsunami watches and warnings, coastal National Weather Service (NWS) offices activate the Emergency Alert System (EAS) via NOAA Weather Radio. All broadcasters (TV, AM/FM radio, and cable TV) receive the tsunami EAS message, as well as anyone who has a weather radio receiver (this includes healthcare facilities, schools, businesses, and homes). NOAA Weather Radio also activates the All-Hazard Alert Broadcast (AHAB) units located in remote coastal areas, alerting people in isolated locations.

Where Do the Watches and Warnings Come From?

Two tsunami warning centers look for earthquakes and any indications that a tsunami might have been generated. If they pick up evidence of a tsunami, they issue watches and warnings for their assigned areas.

The West Coast/Alaska Tsunami Warning Center in Palmer, Alaska, covers California, Oregon, Washingon, Alaska, and British Columbia.

The Pacific Tsunami Warning Center in Ewa Beach, Hawaii, covers the Aloha State as well as all other American territories in the Pacific. It also serves as the International Tsunami Warning Center for twenty-five other member countries in the Pacific Ocean Basin.

If you live on the coast, make an evacuation plan, keep it updated, and be

ready to use it. There's nothing you can do to stop a tsunami, but you can be ready with the right response when "Tommy Tsunami" pays you a visit!

I Dunno Where I'm Gonna Go When the Volcano Blows!

When I think of a volcano, the first image that comes to mind is a large, tall mountain with orange fire and lava spewing out of the top. Ka-boom! Volcanoes *can* explode violently, destroying everything within a few miles of the eruption in a matter of minutes. But there are many volcanoes where the lava seeps out so slowly that you can actually safely walk around them! The severity of a volcano's eruption depends on the thickness and composition of its magma.

A volcano is an opening, vent, or rupture in the surface of the planet that allows material from inside the Earth to escape. When watching an erupting volcano, many of us may

Mount St. Helens volcano, Washington

feel the same emotions as people in ancient times who believed volcanoes were supernatural beings. We stand in awe of this force of nature and are unnerved that what was once a peaceful mountain with pretty snow on top, has been transformed into a raging beast throwing a horrendous, molten magma, fire-spewing fit!

That was the case when Mount St. Helens in the state of Washington erupted in 1980; it had not erupted for 123 years. Most people thought Mount St. Helens was a beautiful, peaceful mountain, not a dangerous volcano.

Volcanoes are generally found where tectonic plates meet violently—where they are pulled apart or jammed together. Volcanoes are rarely found where two tectonic plates slide past each other.

Worldwide, there are 1,500 active—that's right, *active*—volcanoes. Six hundred of those are on the land and the rest are on the ocean floor. All the volcanoes of the world, active, dormant, or extinct, are important because volcanoes make up 80 percent of the Earth's surface.

Hot Magma, Baby!

When magma seeps or blasts onto the Earth's surface, it's called *lava*. How explosive an eruption is depends on how runny or sticky the magma is. If magma is thin and runny, gases easily escape from it. When this type of magma erupts, it flows out of the volcano. Magma that's thick and sticky doesn't flow easily and blocks the gases from escaping. Pressure builds up until the gases escape violently and explode. In this type of eruption, the magma blasts into the air and breaks apart into pieces called *tephra*. Tephra can range in size from tiny particles of ash to house-size boulders!

Explosive volcanic eruptions can be dangerous and deadly. Clouds of hot tephra can blast out from the side or top of a volcano. When Mount St. Helens erupted, the top blew clean off the mountain and fiery clouds raced down the mountainside, destroying everything in their path.

Volcanic ash falls back to Earth as if it were powdery snow, but of course it doesn't melt. If the ashfall is thick enough, it can suffocate plants, animals, and humans. When hot volcanic materials mix with water from streams or melted snow and ice, mudflows are formed. Mudflows can be as dangerous as lava flows. They have buried entire communities near erupting volcanoes.

Where Do These Bad Boys Come From?

Like earthquakes, volcanoes exist because of the rigid plates in the Earth's crust. There are sixteen major plates that float on a softer layer of rock in the Earth's mantle. Most volcanoes occur near the edges of plates.

Sometimes when plates push together, one plate slides beneath the other. This is called a *subduction zone*. When the plunging plates get deep enough inside the mantle, some of the rock on the overlying plate melts and forms magma that can move upward and erupt at the Earth's surface.

At rift zones, where plates are moving apart, magma can reach the surface and erupt. Some volcanoes occur in the middle of plates at areas called *hot spots*—places where magma melts through the plate.

These Guys Must Be on Steroids!

Repeated eruptions cause volcanoes to grow. There are three main shapes of volcanoes based on the stuff that comes out of them when they erupt.

Stratovolcanoes are built from eruptions of lava and tephra that pile up in layers like cake and frosting. They form volcanoes with symmetrical cones and steep sides.

Cinder cone volcanoes are created by erupting lava that breaks into small pieces as it blasts into the air. As the lava pieces fall back to the ground, they cool and harden into cinders that pile up around the volcano's vent. Cinder cones are very small, cone-shape volcanoes.

Shield volcanoes are formed by eruptions of flowing lava. The lava spreads out and builds up volcanoes with broad, gently sloping sides. The shape resembles a warrior's shield.

Here Are a Few of the Most Famous Volcanic Faces!

COTOPAXI, ECUADOR (19,347 FEET/5,897 METERS)

One of the world's tallest active volcanoes, Cotopaxi has erupted more than fifty times since its first recorded eruption in 1534.

ETNA, ITALY (10,902 FEET/3,323 METERS)

With more than two hundred recorded eruptions, Mount Etna is one of Europe's most active volcanoes.

KRAKATAU, INDONESIA (2,667 FEET/813 METERS)

The great eruption of 1883 was heard 2,900 miles away. Enormous sea waves from tsunamis killed 36,000 people.

PARICUTÍN, MEXICO (8,990 FEET/2,740 METERS)

The first volcano to be scientifically observed from its earliest stage of formation, Paricutín began as a small fracture in a farmer's field in 1943.

SURTSEY, ICELAND (568 FEET/173 METERS)

Underwater eruptions created the island of Surtsey, which appeared above the surface of the sea in 1963. Surtsey is now a square mile in area.

VESUVIUS, ITALY (4,203 FEET/1,281 METERS)

The famous eruption in AD 79 destroyed the cities of Pompeii, Stabiae, and Herculaneum.

Nasty, Gnarly, and Naughty Pacific Northwest Winds!

In the hurricane section, I mentioned the book that I think is probably the best weather novel ever written (besides *Category* 7 by Bill Evans and Marianna Jameson!): *Storm* by George R. Stewart. Stewart, a professor of English at the University of California, Berkeley, wrote about a nasty storm referred to as "Maria." While "Maria" was a nasty fictional storm, some nasty, gnarly, *real* storms frequently strike the northwestern Pacific Coast of the United States.

Residents in that area of the country never experience a hurricane or a tornado, but they are battered by giant storms called *extra-tropical lows* that rival any hurricane. An extra-tropical low is basically your everyday low-pressure system, except it grows to be extremely large and dangerous. It's a low-pressure system on steroids!

Some major Pacific Northwest storms have been stronger and caused more damage than a lot of hurricanes. Extra-tropical lows can match a Category 3 hurricane in both minimum central pressures and sustained wind speeds. Such storms have a reach far beyond that of a typical hurricane: they can throw a cold rain into the Alaska Panhandle while pummeling the San Francisco Bay Area with a warm, saturated gale.

Some of these storms have been given very cool names. A couple of the biggest blasts to strike the Pacific Northwest are the "Storm King of 1880" and the "Columbus Day 'Big Blow' of 1962." The term *blowdown* is used to describe a record Northwest windstorm, one that knocks over 1 billion or more board feet of timber. Some blowdowns have wiped out more than 10 billion board feet.

Damage caused by the Columbus Day "Big Blow"

These blowdowns happen every 30 to 40 years. The 1962 Columbus Day storm was the last big blowdown; it destroyed 11 to 15 million board feet of timber. That's an awfully large number of trees!

Not only do these storms have Category 3 hurricane-force winds, they also produce tons of rain and snow. During the "Storm King of 1880," some areas received 4 feet of snow, causing roofs to collapse!

You Are My Sunshine, My *Only* Sunshine!

There would be no "us" if it were not for the sun. I worship the sun just as many ancient cultures did. The sun warms the Earth, makes plants grow, makes the weather, and is absolutely necessary for life.

Scientists say the sun is more than 4.5 billion years old, and will last billions more. The sun is a star just like the ones we see at night—except it's a lot closer. Like all stars, the sun is a collection of gases, mainly helium and hydrogen, and works like a giant nuclear reactor.

The sun's core is a nuclear furnace where gravity pulls all mass inward, creating immense pressure. That pressure causes nuclear fusion reactions between hydrogen atoms, which then become helium atoms. These reactions give off a huge amount of heat, estimated at 27 million degrees.

☼INSIDE THE SUN☼

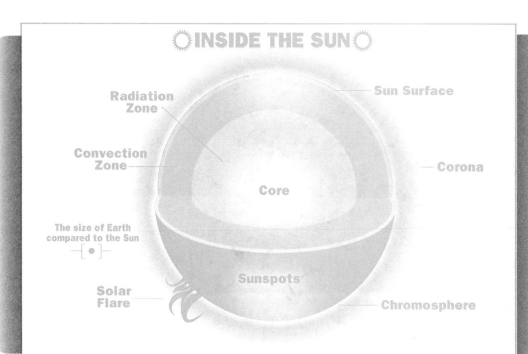

Radiation Zone

Sun Surface

Convection Zone

Corona

Core

The size of Earth compared to the Sun

Solar Flare

Sunspots

Chromosphere

The radiation zone is the layer above the core where energy is carried outward by gamma rays. Hydrogen and other atoms absorb and emit gamma rays millions of times, and the energy from that cycle is transformed into ultraviolet light.

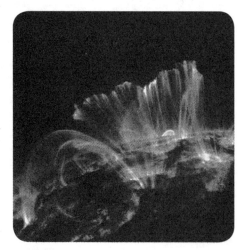

The convection zone is the outermost 30 percent of the sun. It is dominated by convection currents that carry energy to the surface. It's sort of like when you open a bottle of club soda and the bubbles race to the top.

The layer of the sun we see is the photosphere, the temperature of which is about 11,000°F (6,093°C). It appears bubbly, like the simmering surface of a pot of water.

The chromosphere lies above the surface of the sun, but we can't see it because of the photosphere's brightness. It's believed that convection is caused in the chromosphere due to the underlying photosphere, resulting in 180,000 degrees of heat!

The corona is the final layer of the sun. It extends several million miles out from the photosphere and is most noticeable in X-rays of the sun and during solar eclipses. The corona is the white part around the sun you see in an eclipse. Scientists believe that the magnetism of the sun enables the corona to reach its amazing temperature of 5 million degrees Fahrenheit (2,777,760°C)!

Sunspots, the cool dark areas on the sun, are intense magnetic fields. They can be five times the size of the Earth. They are a little cooler than the photosphere at 7,600°F (4,204°C)! Sunspots always appear in pairs and come in 11-year cycles called the *solar cycle.*

The Light, the Light, I Can't Stop Moving Toward the Light!

Solar flares are violent explosions that are caused by sudden changes in the sun's magnetic field. Flares are made up of ultraviolet light, X-rays, gas, and electrons. When this blast of

radiation hits the Earth's magnetic field, it interacts with the North and South poles to produce the aurora borealis. Solar flares disrupt communications, satellites, navigation systems, and power grids. They've even caused blackouts!

Hey, That Cloud Looks Like a Pony!

Did you know you can forecast the weather by looking at the clouds? You can! Some clouds indicate fair and beautiful weather, while others indicate trouble ahead.

I love looking at clouds. You should go outside, to a yard, a patio, a deck, or a big open field, lie on your back, and look at the sky.

I will never forget the time I freaked out my four kids while we were at the beach because I knew the clouds. I didn't know the clouds personally, I just knew what different clouds meant. You can, too!

We were at Greenwich Beach in Connecticut, when I noticed a cumulonimbus cloud whose updrafts were starting to billow the cloud up into the summer sky. The cloud was situated over land to our east, and as the hot summer day wore on, I noticed that the cloud was starting to drift a bit westward, toward us. The sun was behind us, keeping everything bright and hot, and no one else noticed the cloud in the haze above Long Island Sound.

I gathered the kids together and said, "We have to get to the car, it's going to blast down rain in about two minutes." In total disbelief, eyes rolling, my wife and kids picked up the beach chairs and towels, and headed for the car. No one else was leaving the beach but us. Just as we got everything and everyone in the car, *Ka-boom, Blammo, Ker-Pow!* Lightning cracked the sky, a big clap of thunder sent a shock wave over the beach, and a torrent of rain fell from the "cumulo-monster." People were screaming and running from the beach. About 10 minutes later, when my family picked their jaws up off the floor of the car, a faint voice asked, "How did you know that?"

Rapunzel, Let Down Thy Locks of Cirrus So I May Climb to the Sky!

To me, cirrus clouds are the most beautiful of all clouds. Their name comes from the Latin for "lock of hair" and they are delicate wisps of ice that appear high in the heavens. They are the highest of the ten main cloud types at 24,000 feet. Some of the wisps have curls or hooks, and look like what's called *mare's tails*. Cirrus clouds tell us there is going to be fair weather and little in the way to block the sun!

Amber Waves of Clouds . . .

Billow clouds look like ocean waves. They are generally created by wind shear, which occurs either when winds at different levels are blowing in slightly different directions, or are of different strengths. The turbulent, rotary motion between the waves gives them their unique look.

That Is One Bad Mama Jama!

Cumulonimbus clouds are the monsters of the midway. They are also called *thunderheads*. They are the king of the cloud jungle and can tower as high as 55,000 to 60,000 feet. Really nasty ones, called super cells, can create life-threatening conditions. Gusty straight-line winds, flooding rains, lightning, hail, and tornadoes are the usual suspects with these bad boys.

Dude, I See a Martian in That Cloud!

Lenticular clouds are the favorites of the UFO crowd. They are shaped like spaceships and many people who believe in aliens think these clouds are formed by alien spaceships. Lenticular clouds are really formed when a stable layer of air is forced to rise over hills or mountain peaks.

Their smoothness is quite striking, and upon close examination, you can see they form on the leading edge of a mountain and dissipate on the downward side of a mountain.

That Leprechaun Dude Is Lurking!!

Rainbows are one of the most gorgeous meteorological phenomena. When I see them, it gives me a warm feeling of goodness and hope; I know that all is right with the world.

Rainbows appear when the sun is behind us and falling rain is in front of us. The rainbow's spectrum is caused by sunlight shining through raindrops or droplets of moisture. The light is refracted as it enters the surface of the raindrop, then reflected off the back of the drop, and refracted again as it leaves the drop.

The colors of the rainbow are, beginning at the top, red, orange, yellow, green, blue, indigo, and violet. Very rarely, a secondary rainbow is seen, a touch fainter with the colors in the opposite order, with violet on the top and red on the

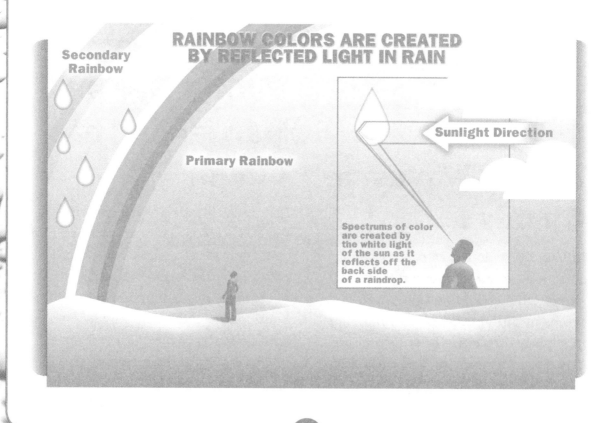

RAINBOW COLORS ARE CREATED BY REFLECTED LIGHT IN RAIN

Secondary Rainbow

Primary Rainbow

Sunlight Direction

Spectrums of color are created by the white light of the sun as it reflects off the back side of a raindrop.

bottom. I saw this once myself in the mountains of Tucson, Arizona. The two rainbows were awesome looking!

A rainbow is an optical illusion whose apparent position in the sky depends on the observer's location. You can make a rainbow at home with the garden sprinkler; just make sure you make the drops very small or a mist.

Eyes on the Skies!

The question I am asked the most has to be, "How do you know it's going to rain?" It's a great question with an easy answer!

I have two wonderful tools: Weather satellites in outer space and Doppler radars on the ground are our eyes on the skies.

The first weather satellite was launched on April 1, 1960 (that's right, April Fool's Day, but this was no joke!). Its name was TIROS-I. Compared to today's satellites, it was pretty crude, equipped with what amounted to a Brownie camera and an AM transmitter! But TIROS-I represented the dawn of a new era. For the first time, meteorologists could see pictures of a storm over the northeastern United States.

Nowadays, satellites carry instruments, not cameras, that scan the Earth to form images. Geostationary Operational Environmental Satellites (GOES) circle the Earth at a very high altitude of 22,500 miles in what's called a *geostationary* orbit. That means they always stay above the same part of the Earth's surface, for instance observing the Northern Hemisphere. The instruments on these satellites detect and measure

the Earth's emitted radiation, from which atmospheric temperature, wind direction and speed, moisture, and cloud cover can be derived. GOES data are used to generate the satellite animations that you see on television. The first geostationary satellite (GOES-1) was launched on October 16, 1975, and quickly became a critical part of our weather forecasting.

Polar Operational Environmental Satellites (POES) operate on polar orbits at a low altitude of about 500 miles high near the North and South poles. The polar orbit allows the satellite to provide complete coverage of the Earth as the planet turns beneath the satellite. TRIOS-I

was a POES satellite.

My second most important tool is Doppler radar. Radar is an acronym for *radio detection and ranging.* Christian Andreas Doppler was an Austrian physicist who, in 1842, first described how the observed frequency of light and sound waves was affected by the relative motion of the source and the detector. This phenomenon became known as the *Doppler effect.*

A radar antenna sends out short, high-powered bursts of radio wave energy of approximately 1,000 pulses per second. Radar uses radio waves at the very high end of the radio spectrum. After each pulse, the radar listens for a signal reflected back from the cloud. When the pulse hits any precipitation—rain, snow, or ice—the energy of the pulse is scattered, so only a small part of the signal returns to the antenna.

The radar measures the strength of the received signal and how long it takes to return from the cloud, which tells meteorologists how far away the precipitation is. This area of the radar is called *base reflectivity.* Doppler radar can tell you how hard the rain, snow, or ice is falling, as well as its position and height. Precipitation images are updated every 4 to 6 minutes.

Weather radar systems use colors

to indicate the intensity of precipitation. Light blues indicate light rain and the colors go up from shades of blues to yellows to reds as the rain or snow grows stronger and denser. If you see red on a Doppler radar, you need to find a safe shelter!

You're a Big Windbag!

The other beautiful feature of Doppler radar is that it can see turbulence. The vertical velocity feature of the radar allows us to pick out areas of a thunderstorm where violent, rotating winds may indicate that a tornado's funnel cloud might be forming.

This happened to me just a few years ago while I was doing the weather live on-air. I suddenly saw, in a line of thunderstorms I was showing, a little group of colors that represented a comma or hook shape. I immediately knew it was a funnel cloud. The shape was moving from Staten Island across New York Harbor toward Brooklyn. I warned Brooklyn residents to not go outside as they might encounter a tornado. Luckily, no one was injured, but an EF1 tornado touched down several times and caused a lot of damage to brownstone buildings and town houses, and knocked over trees.

Who Thought Up the Word *Meteorologist*?

The Greek philosopher Aristotle is one of my heroes. He is credited with discovering many scientific things. For me personally, his greatest discovery is what he termed *Meteorologica*, the first major study of the atmosphere. From Aristotle's work came the term *meteorologist*, meaning a person who studies the atmosphere.

I honestly believe that I have never worked a day in my life. Each day I wake, I can't wait to take a look at the weather. I look forward to going to the weather office every day, even when I get the forecast wrong! That's the beauty of weather forecasting: when you make a forecast and the next day the weather looks nothing like what you forecasted, then you know exactly what you did wrong!

I even look at the weather when I'm not going to the office. So I guess it's true that if you love what you do for a living, you will have never worked a day in your life, because it's not work, it's a pleasure.

I have lots of weather jobs. I do the weather on TV, digital cable, radio, and the Web. I teach meteorology as well. It's weather, weather, weather, all the time! I love it!

Performing the weather on television is fun, but it carries with it a big responsibility. I know that some people think weathermen are only good for telling you whether or not you need to wear a coat or carry an umbrella, but forecasting means much more than that.

It is my job to inform you and all my viewers and listeners about what type of weather to expect, and if there is going to be any dangerous or life-threatening weather nearby. I view the meteorologist's role as that of a public servant. I help people plan their days when things are normal and let them know if they need to take drastic measures such as evacuating from their home, school, or workplace. Accurate forecasts help people at times of crisis, but also in their everyday lives.

I love helping people—and sometimes people ask for my help with the most interesting things! Once a lady called me and said she wanted me to come to her home and take a look at a meteor that had crashed through the trunk of her car. I tried to explain to her that was work for an astronomer and she began yelling at me, "But you call yourself a 'me-te-or-ol-o-gist!'"

The most interesting part of my job is going on camera. When you see a meteorologist doing the weather on TV, he or she is not standing in front of a real weather map. The meteorologist is standing in front of a blue or green wall. In weather reporting, we use a technique called *chroma key.*

Chroma key allows us to mix two images together by removing a specific color from one image, revealing the second image behind the first. Blue and green are used most often because they are the least

like skin tone. Sometimes when blue is used, people's shirts and ties disappear! They look pretty funny with the weather maps right under their chins. For this reason, the wall behind me on the WABC-TV set is bright green.

The weather computer, video, still pictures, and any other images we are going to use are all keyed to that shade of green. Once on Halloween, I wore a green bodysuit that covered everything except my face. I was completely invisible! I looked like a floating head! This is the same technique used in movies to make characters look invisible or to place them in fantastic, computer-created settings.

What is often called *bluescreen technology* was invented in 1940 by Larry Butler. One of the first movies to use bluescreen technology was 1958's *The Old Man and the Sea*, starring Spencer Tracy.

I Know the Story: You Walked to School Every Day, Uphill Both Ways, in the Snow!

When I started in TV, the weather computer hadn't been invented yet. I did the weather standing in front of physical maps. The weather symbols I used were either magnets or pieces of thin, soft plastic, which I wetted and stuck to the map. Once, during a live weathercast, someone turned on a fan in the studio and blew all my symbols off the map!

Some weathercasters would use a marker to draw the fronts and symbols right onto the map or onto a piece of glass that had the map drawn on it. These guys were so good they could stand behind the glass and draw the weather systems backward! When you watched them, it looked completely normal because they were so comfortable working backward!

Computerized weather graphics came along in the 1970s and revolutionized the way the weather was presented. Weathercasters could now show radar and satellite pictures, animated loops, weather maps, temperature charts, and even graphics that explained the weather. It was a very exciting time! Now we could actually show what the weather was doing! We could also show what we expected the weather to do. Everything was easier—it was easier for us to explain the weather

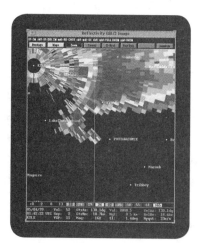

and easier for viewers to understand what was going on.

Dude, Do You Know You're Talking to a Green Wall?

I always get asked, "How do you know what you're pointing to when you stand in front of a blank green wall?"

I always answer, "Practice, practice, practice," which, of course, is also how you get to Carnegie Hall! When I look at the barren optic green screen, I can also see TV monitors to either side of the wall. I can see myself and the images behind me.

It definitely does take a little practice to know where you are pointing. Sometimes when I have a group of students on the set, I'll let them try it. Nearly every time, someone says, "Here's California," while pointing at Florida!

My favorite prank to play on someone new to the TV business (or on one of my interns) is to ask them if they wouldn't mind getting the "chroma key" from the newsroom. This starts off a chain reaction in the building as everyone at work is familiar with this ingenious form of torture and is in on my little joke.

"Do you have the chroma key?" asks the naïve little innocent. "Why, you know, I don't, but I think Bob on the assignment desk does," says a person who is struggling to keep from bursting with laughter. Bob sends the victim to someone else, who then sends them to someone else, and so on. Finally, when they have been exhausted by this find-the-chroma-key-quest, they end up back in the boss's office . . . and I then kindly explain the weather department's little form of pseudosadism! It's all in fun and everybody gets a good laugh. Plus, it teaches a great lesson about the "chroma key"!

How Do I Get a Job in This Biz?

In a recent survey by the *Jobs Ranked Almanac*, the career of meteorologist was ranked seventh out of 250 jobs. Woo hoo! I knew being a meteorologist was fun! The rankings are based on factors including environment, security, stress, income, employment outlook, and physical demands.

What's great about the field is that you have many careers to choose from. You can work in broadcasting, like me, or choose from a number of other weather-related jobs that are just as exciting and rewarding, from taking weather instrument observations to working with supercomputers. You can work for many federal agencies, including the CIA and the military; in private meteorology; for local or state government; for universities, utility companies, engineering consulting firms, or Wall Street.

If you love weather, are curious about the world around you, like science and math, and wish to work in a field where things can change in an instant, then meteorology is for you!

First, you are going to need a college degree in atmospheric science or meteorology. More than one hundred universities, large and small, offer undergraduate and graduate degrees in atmospheric or related sciences in the United States and Canada. In addition, the American Meteorological Society has an online weather course that has been licensed by three hundred colleges and universities across the country.

You don't have to study meteorology to contribute to the

field. There are a lot of physicists and computer scientists in meteorology. A degree in math, science, chemistry, or physics is highly regarded as well.

Some cool meteorology jobs are not on TV or radio. You could be a forensic meteorologist. Let's say an insurance company needs to find out, "Was this house destroyed by a tornado or straight-line winds?" A forensic meteorologist might be hired to investigate the case. You'd have to do a lot of research and amazing science, and you might even be called on to testify in a court of law. I have done that myself and I can tell you, it's *very* exciting.

I was asked to be an expert witness in a case involving the newly built home of the wealthiest person in the town where I was doing the weather on TV. A hurricane had damaged his home and the owner was suing the contractor who had built the house. The owner was saying that the damage done by heavy rains was due in large part to a poor construction job. He contended that the cedar-shingled roof and cedar-tile walls leaked.

The lawyer who was representing the contractor took me to see the damage and asked for my expert assessment. This is the exact job of a forensic meteorologist and that made

me, Bill Evans, Forensics Man! I examined the damage, examined the building, and took a tour of the neighborhood. I went back to my office and researched the hurricane, which was named Elena. (Look up that hurricane and you will know where I was!) I checked at the wind pattern, the amount of rain, and the path of the storm.

As it turned out, the culprit was the direction of the wind and the path it took between the houses near the wealthy guy's home. The wind was funneled in such a way that it sent rain and wind underneath the eaves of the roof of this beautiful, brand-new, cedar-tiled home. I know you're asking, "What about insurance?" The house's owner did not have flood insurance, and his homeowner's insurance company was skeptical. Plus, the homeowner was really angry. He wanted to obliterate the guy who had built his new, leaky house.

But it was actually the architect who was at fault—his design was flawed. I had figured it out! I had enough evidence to keep the contractor who built the home from losing a fortune and having his career tarnished.

This was only the beginning of my adventure. I had to testify on the witness stand, in court, against a guy who had so much money he could have bought me ten times over!

On trial day, I was taken to the witness room, where all those who have to testify must sit and wait to be called. It was a big room with dark, wood floors and tall windows in an old-style federal courthouse. Sitting there, all alone in the room, I thought, "I wish I were in the Witness Protection Program!"

"Mr. Evans, time to go see the judge," boomed the very deep voice of the bailiff. It's the bailiff's job to run the court for the judge.

After swearing to tell the truth, I had to answer all kinds of questions from the lawyers for both sides while the richest guy in town stared me down from his chair. His piercing, ice-blue eyes gave me the creeps! After I'd explained the basics of how hurricanes work and answered all the lawyers' questions, the judge spoke. "So, Mr. Evans, tell the court: In your best opinion, what was the reason for all the flood damage to the home?"

I explained to the judge that the rich dude's home faced south and the two nearby houses faced west. There was a grove of trees on each side. As Hurricane Elena traveled east to west, the winds in this area were out of the east to northeast and were channeled between the two houses and the tree grove. This acted like a shotgun blast, sending rain and wind into the home in question since the eaves underneath the roof were built open, which was the norm in that part of the country. It was my opinion that the water damage was due to geological and design reasons. The whole time I was talking, I was shaking like crazy on the inside! "Thank you for your expert testimony today, Mr. Evans. You are dismissed," said the judge kindly.

As I was walking down the hall to leave, I felt a tap on my shoulder. "You did a fine job." I turned around and it was the rich dude, who was looking at me with those eyes that seem to fire an ice-blue laser beam right through my stomach!

"Thanks," I said.

The rich guy lost—but he also won in the end. He was able to work out a settlement with the architect whose design had failed. It was a great experience for me, and I learned a lot about what a forensic meteorologist has to do.

What Other Kinds of Work Can I Do?

There's private industrial forecasting. You might work for a private company or you might work as a consultant who does forecasting for many businesses. A ski resort might need help with snowmaking. You might forecast the weather for a film production company planning to shoot on an outdoor set, or for the cruise ship industry. You might be hired by utility companies to provide warnings of storms that might damage their equipment or cause service interruptions.

You could work for the federal government, for the National Weather Service or for the National Oceanic and Atmospheric Administration. NOAA has a number of really cool ships that travel the world doing research and undersea mapping. How cool would it be to travel all over the world and study the atmosphere or the ocean!

I Want to Be the Donald Trump of Meteorology!

One area that is really growing is forecasting for Wall Street firms.

I once had an intern named Rob, who decided he did not want to work in broadcasting. After he finished meteorology school, Rob took a job with a Wall Street investment firm, forecasting weather for the commodities section. Rob would give the traders long-range weather forecasts, and they would use the information to guide their purchases of commodities like corn, wheat, coffee, sugar, and cocoa.

Rob's forecasts projected weather conditions 120 days into the future. If he predicted floods or a drought— any kind of bad weather that could destroy crops—the brokers he worked with would buy hundreds of tons of wheat or corn before the bad weather hit. Then, with less wheat or corn available in the marketplace due to bad weather, the firm would make a lot of money when they sold the crops. At the end of Rob's first year with his firm, he got a huge cash bonus. He was quite excited and was certainly happy with his career choice!

There are other interesting Wall Street connections, such as a hedge fund I know of that operates in hurricanes. Basically, the fund tries to figure out where the next hurricane will hit. Then it invests its clients' money in companies that will benefit from the storm. For instance, the fund might invest in a home-improvement company such as Home Depot and make their money when the company's stock rises when it sells a lot of building supplies before or after a damaging hurricane.

As you can see, there are plenty of different kinds of weather-related jobs.

I like the fact that there is a large public service component to meteorology. It is a great, rewarding job because you educate the public and help protect society. You are helping people become more aware of natural hazards.

I really hope that one day we will be colleagues in this great field of science we call meteorology!

Some Great Web Sites! >>>>

Lightning

http://sky-fire.tv/index.cgi/lightning.html#harness

Flooding

http://pubs.water.usgs.gov/fs2004-3060/ (flood mapping before it happens)

http://waterdata.usgs.gov/nwis/rt/ (stream flow information)

www.floodsmart.gov/floodsmart/

Drought

www.drought.unl.edu/dm/monitor.html.

Tsunamis

www.tidesandcurrents.noaa.gov/

www.prh.noaa.gov/itic

Detection Buoys

www.ndbc.noaa.gov/dart.shtml

www.prh.noaa.gov/ptwc/

Subscribe for Tsunami Alerts

http://ioc3.unesco.org/itic/
contents.php?id=142

. Illustrations .

The author is indebted to the National Oceanic and Atmospheric Administration, the U.S. Geological Survey, NASA, the National Science Foundation, and FEMA, which make information and images readily available to the public via their Web sites: www.noaa.gov, www.usgs.gov, www.nasa.gov, www.nsf.gov, and www.fema.gov. Without the work done by these scientists and engineers, and without their desire to educate and inform, we would all know a lot less about our world.

Page 3: National Oceanic and Atmospheric Administration/Department of Commerce; Photographer: Joey Ketcham

Pages 4, 6, 8-10, 15-17, 19, 23, 33, 42, 43, 49, 67, 68 (both), 72, 74, 75, 81 (bottom), 106-114, 117, 127, 141 (both), 152, 166 (both), 168, 171 (right), 174, 177, 187, 195, 197, 205: National Oceanic and Atmospheric Administration/Department of Commerce

Pages 6, 7, 18, 27, 44, 46, 47, 50, 94, 104, 105, 116, 165, 206 (top), 210: Frank Picini

Page 22: National Oceanic and Atmospheric Administration/Department of Commerce; Photographer: Steve Nicklas

Page 27: Fred K. Smith; used by permission.

Page 36: Christian Oneto Gaona; used by permission.

Pages 41, 192 (all), 199, 200: U.S. Geological Survey/Department of the Interior

Pages 49 (both), 55, 57 (top), 61, 154, 206 (bottom), 207, 211, 212: NASA

Pages 57 (bottom), 83, 85 (both), 87, 89 (both), 90, 91, 93: National Hurricane Center, National Weather Service, National Oceanic and Atmospheric Administration/Department of Commerce

Page 59: Mike Irwin; used by permission.

Page 81 (top): National Oceanic and Atmospheric Administration/Department of Commerce; Photographer: Dewie Floyd

Pages 101, 142, 143, 204: National Weather Service, National Oceanic and Atmospheric Administration/Department of Commerce

Page 115: used by permission of James Quirk; taken by his grandfather.

Page 120 (top): United States Antarctic Program, National Science Foundation; Photographer: Jerrod Clausen

Pages 120 (bottom), 121, 122: Bill Adler; used by permission.

Page 134: FEMA/Andrea Booher

Pages 139-140, 163: Currier & Ives

Pages 157 and 158: Fritz Grueter; used by permission.

Page 164: Julie Rozzi; used by permission.

Page 169: Kid Gizmo; used by permission.

Page 171 (left): David Dewhurst; used by permission.

Page 172: Kumalie Walker; used by permission.

Page 173: Realine Media; used by permission.

Page 175: David Sobotta; used by permission.

Page 186: Sydney Oats; used by permission.

Page 191: FEMA/Dane Golden

Pages 214-215: Steve Fenn; used by permission.